WHAT PEOPLE ARE SAYING ABOUT
THE MOST
VALUABLE CATCH

"Countless books have been written on the subject of leadership, with authors often resorting to overused slogans and outdated illustrations. Steve Jamison's book, *The Most Valuable Catch*, offers a fresh approach to a timeless topic. This book will inspire you—and stretch you—to be more like Jesus. On a scale of 1-10, this is a 10."

—Hal Donaldson
President, Convoy of Hope

"Steve Jamison is a seasoned leader and trusted voice. When you hit storms at sea, and you will, this book will help anchor you to God. The lessons Steve shares are tried and true."

—Mark Batterson
NYT bestselling author, The Circle Maker

"As a friend, mentor and brother, I've had the pleasure of serving with Steve Jamison for over 20 years. His passionate pursuit of truth, his humble approach, and authenticity have been the Christ-like qualities that I admire in him and his ministry. I know you will love *The Most Valuable Catch*! God will speak dreams into your heart in a mighty way!"

—Allan Houston
2x NBA All-Star, Olympic gold medalist
Founder of FISLL, Knicks Executive

"For over 25 years, I have had the privilege and pleasure of having a friend that has stuck closer than a brother. Even though we have been raised in different parts of the country, with very different backgrounds and from different cultures, God had bonded us in a very unique manner. Our relationship and friendship have extended to our families and our ministries. Steve Jamison's insights will empower you, inspire you and educate you in powerful ways. I encourage you to dive into *The Most Valuable Catch* and be blessed."

—*John K. Jenkins, Sr.*
Senior Pastor, First Baptist Church of Glenarden

"Steve Jamison has just released a **One-Of-A-Kind Book** that could only be written by a **One-Of-A-Kind Leader!** From a crazy (wait till you read it!) high-adventure childhood straight from the *Deadliest Catch*, to preaching NBA style arena events, to launching one of Seattle's largest and highest impact churches—Steve is a unicorn! Steve's first book, *The Most Valuable Catch*, is impossible to put down. I've never read anything like it because no Christian book has ever been like it. From nearly being lost at sea, crazy midnight shark stories and 20-hour dangerous days, it's like reading a scary, crazy and dangerous account of Alaskan fishing … AND a brilliant call to live a life of vibrant faith and world changing impact. For a generation living in fear, Steve's book is a compelling call to launch into a life of living confidently and leading boldly! It's about time!"

—*Ray Johnston*
President Thriving Church Intl.
Senior Lead Pastor, Bayside Church

"Steve Jamison has written a book filled with truth! Truth about his life experiences. Truth about God's word and the power of it. Truth about how to listen, integrate, apply God's word, and experience the adventure of a lifetime. His story as a follower of Christ will stir your heart to "head for deeper water" and be fully alive in the sea of humanity. He shares these truths so you can effectively impact the people's lives you engage with."

—*Anne Beiler*
Founder of Auntie Anne's Soft Pretzels,
Author and public speaker

"Steve Jamison is absolutely one of the biggest dreamers I have ever known and he has seen seemingly impossible dreams actually come to fruition. From filling the largest venues, such as Madison Square Garden, to bringing together NBA players and top Christian Ministries, to building one of the largest and most influential churches in America, he has successfully used *The Most Valuable Catch* to change multitudes of lives. As a friend of many years, I have been privileged to have a front row seat to the life and ministry of this great man. *The Most Valuable Catch* is a must read! It is a 100% life changer!"

—*Tommy Barnett*
Dream City Church, Phoenix
Dream Center, Los Angeles

"A great privilege of my life was to standing side-by-side Steve, serving and assisting him and his team who were themselves serving the pastors in Washington D.C. through the Jammin' events! I witnessed first-hand the steps of faith God set before Steve and how he listened and responded. What a journey that is! Every challenge and problem genuinely became an opportunity to see what God would do to provide and direct. That is a life lived by faith and not by sight . . . the abundant life. As a young believer, I wanted to live that life! Steve and Cheryl modeled it, and it gave me the courage and the principles I could follow. And the result—many souls saved and the unity of the Body further established. What a blessing. And even more, the establishment of a lifelong friendship between Steve and myself! Don't go on another day without capturing and applying these principles for yourself. You can likewise encourage those around you. Like all things of the Lord, it's not only for your own good, it will begin to flow out of your life to those around you . . . like rivers of living water."

—*Andrew Palau*
Evangelist and author

"Steve Jamison has written a powerful new book called *Most Valuable Catch* that gives you inspiration, information, and wise insights on how you can transform your life using proven principles! He went from working with his father, on a boat as a fisherman, to becoming a fisher of people. He has gone on to change the lives of millions with his arena rallies and his messages at his church and online, where people around the globe have been inspired by his thinking and his passion for uplifting others through biblical principles! I highly recommend you read this book, then re-read it and then share it with everyone you know! They will be blessed and you will be blessed, because you will be an example of the *Most Valuable Catch*!"

—*Dr. Willie Jolley,*
Hall of Fame Speaker, Sirius XM Radio Show Host
and Best Selling Author of A Setback Is A Setup For
A Comeback & An Attitude of Excellence

"I always appreciate when an author writes from reality rather than perspective. Steve Jamison has provided a book full of tools that builds the church and calls for people to follow and love their leaders. From small groups to staff training, *The Most Valuable Catch* is a book well worth journeying through."

—*Doug Clay*
General Superintendent, Assemblies of God US

"Hi Everybody, this is Rick Rizzs of the Seattle Mariners and you're going to love *The Most Valuable Catch* by Pastor Steve. Our Lord was a fisher of men and now we're hearing inspirational stories from Pastor Steve fishing with his father looking for a bounty under the water while saving so many lives above it by bringing people to Christ! You'll be entertained and moved every step of the way, chapter by chapter! If you're looking for a closer relationship with our Lord with your two feet on the ground, spend some time with Pastor Steve on a boat!"

—*Rick Rizzs*
Seattle Mariners lead radio voice

"I'm so grateful for how Steve Jamison has mentored me and also become an amazing friend. His guidance has been instrumental in my career, my marriage, in raising our four children and, most importantly, in my walk with Jesus. As followers of Christ, we are called to equip and pour into the next generation to grow the Kingdom, letting the ripples of His work pass on. In *The Most Valuable Catch*, Steve imparts wisdom from his life journey to equip leaders who desire intimacy with Jesus, while making an eternal impact in the lives of others."

—*Matt Boyd*
MLB starting pitcher, Detroit Tigers

"Steve Jamison is my friend, and he understands fishing and ministry. It is only natural for him to connect the two, and he has done a wonderful job in this book. Steve is a master storyteller, and you will be encouraged and challenged as you read through these pages with very applicable lessons. Jesus has a special place in his heart for fisherman turned ministers."

—*Dr. Donald E. Ross*
NW Ministry Network Leader
Author of Turnaround Pastor

I've never read a book that uses offshore fishing as a metaphor for spiritual tenacity . . . until I read this one by my friend Steve Jamison. You don't have to be a fisherman (or fisherwoman) to find yourself in his stories on the deck of his dad's boat in the gulf of Alaska. In every chapter, he puts us "in the moment," learning the lessons his father taught him. Steve uses these stories to explain how our walk with God is the most fulfilling, exciting life we can imagine, but only if we develop a love for the Captain and learn to respond to His voice. Pick up this book and start reading it. You won't put it down.

—*Scott Wilson*
Global Pastor, Oaks Church, Red Oak, Texas
Author of Identity: The Search for
Significance and True Success

THE MOST VALUABLE CATCH

**RISKING IT
ALL FOR WHAT
MATTERS THE
MOST**

STEVE JAMISON

AVAIL

Cover design by Sara Young
Cover photo by Andrejs Polivanovs
Cover photo ship by Philip Stephen
Author bio photo by Jean Johnson Portraits
Fishing photos by Marvin (Mike) Unverzagt
Safeco Field photo by VanHouten Photography, Inc.
Jammin' photos by Troy Hunt and Fred Baye

ISBN: 978-1-959095-71-2   1 2 3 4 5 6 7 8 9 10

Printed in the United States of America

This book is dedicated to my family.

*To my parents Vern and Pat Jamison whose faith
helped shape my life and planted courage in my soul.*

To my wife Cheryl, you are the love and treasure of my life!

*Thank you for chasing the dreams of God with me and
filling my heart with a lifetime of love and joy!*

*To my son Josh and his wife Carrie, my daughter Janelle
and her husband Brandon, and my son Jordan.*

To the next generation, Trenton, Drew, Liv, and Asher

*God has even greater dreams to live through each
of you. My love and heart are with you!*

*And to our Eastridge Church family; your love, faith, and
support has made the journey of serving you a tremendous
blessing. Keep reaching for the most valuable catch!*

CONTENTS

ACKNOWLEDGMENTS

I want to acknowledge the people who have helped make this project possible—

The board and leadership team of Eastridge Church. Thank you for having the vision to see Eastridge reach beyond our doors to touch the world.

I want to thank Sam Chand and Martijn van Tilborgh for the invitation to partner with AVAIL. Your vision and passion to see the message of *The Most Valuable Catch* build people and change lives has helped make it possible.

I want to thank Pat Springle for his excellence in writing with me. Pat, you are a champion!

A huge thanks to the AVAIL team, John, Debbie, Allison, and Sarah for helping make the vision and message of the book come to life. You have been tremendous partners through the process.

I would like to also thank early readers, Josh Jamison, Dana and Corrine Rand, Janet Bechtel, David Oliphant, and Gail and Darrel Johnsen for your encouragement and insights.

FOREWORD

What is the most crucial aspect of a Christian believer's maturing relationship with God?

It is to hear God. Follow His bidding boldly. Exercise courageous obedience. Live a fulfilled life. Keep listening, following, and obeying for ongoing future direction.

That is what my friend Pastor Steve Jamison will help you discover.

In *The Most Valuable Catch, Steve taught me to hear God's voice*, perceive life through a Kingdom lens, and know that He is for me and with me.

Through Steve's captivating stories on the open seas, I learned that leadership is a sacred trust accompanied by shared responsibility. His insights to building your life and leadership are fresh and practical.

Maybe you are struggling with finding your place in serving the Kingdom of God. Maybe you are searching for ways to utilize the fullness of your life to the glory God. Don't feel alone. That struggle is real. I am continually challenged in this area because God is speaking constantly with new directions and assignments.

In this book, Steve will challenge you to step up and seek God for your next steps—knowing that He is speaking to you, longing for you to hear Him, and calling you to chase after what He has already given to you.

The greatest move of God in your life is waiting for you.

Hear Him.

Follow Him.

Be bold.

Stay courageous.

Live fulfilled.

—Sam Chand

Steve Jamison's friend

INTRODUCTION

When the Discovery Channel launched the show *Deadliest Catch* in 2005, for the first time, people were transported from their warm living rooms to being on the deck of a King Crab boat fishing in the frigid and raging waters of the Bering Sea of Alaska. It not only gave people a great level of respect for the fishermen but also stirred a question for some, "could I make it out there in those conditions?"

I was raised around what many believe are the two most difficult fisheries in the world, King Crabbing and Longline Halibut fishing. My hometown of Anacortes, Washington, was known for being the home of the "A boats," a fleet of state-of-the-art King Crab boats that each season would travel to fish the Bering Sea. My Dad was a halibut and albacore fisherman who would travel to Alaska in early Spring to fish halibut. There has always been a tremendous amount of mutual respect between King Crabbers and open-ocean Halibut fishermen. The King Crabbers faced the most intense weather with freezing temperatures in the dead of winter. My friends who crabbed would talk about wearing goggles because it was blowing eighty miles an hour and hailing at times. The crabbers would give the nod back to us as open ocean Halibut fishermen. Those in the know would often say there is no more intense or grueling work than that which a halibut crew faced in setting 15-20 miles of gear and thousands of hooks every day

You may wonder if fishing in Alaska is really that dangerous or just hype. I can tell you it's for real. In February 1983, two of the King Crab boats from my hometown, the Altair and the Americus, both went down as they headed into the Bering Sea. All fourteen crew members were lost that day. I will never forget the gut-wrenching grief our little town of 9,000 people faced with the loss of these great young men and their captains. I was stunned. That day I lost ten guys I had grown up with and attended High School together. Some people say that even after all these years, the community has not fully recovered from the loss. As sad as the Anacortes tragedy was, they were not the only fishing friends we have lost to the sea.

I have written this book to inspire and equip you to grow your personal life and leadership. I will share real-life principles of how you can discern the voice of God in your life and develop the confidence and courage to untie from the dock and head to deeper water, chasing the dreams God has for you. I am excited to share with you the leadership principles I learned on the deck of my Dad's boat in Alaska. These lessons of teamwork, grit, relationship, and stewardship were instrumental in preparing me to work with professional athletes, business leaders, pastors, ministry leaders, and public officials to hold outreach events in some of our nation's great arenas, such as Madison Square Garden. My prayer is that you will find a fresh perspective and practical tools that will help you lead people through difficult challenges and take your ministry and businesses to greater effectiveness. I am sharing keys that have helped our church grow strong in the challenging spiritual soil of the Pacific Northwest.

I believe God will use these Biblical truths to help you discover what is really the most valuable catch in your life. In other words, what is worth the investment of your heart and soul? You will learn leadership principles that will equip you to not only achieve success in life and ministry, but to build it, sustain it, and leave a lasting legacy.

The title of this book parallels a conversation Jesus had with the Pharisees. In the week before He was arrested, falsely accused, condemned, tortured, and executed, the religious leaders tried their best to make Jesus look foolish, or perhaps uneducated. They set a number of verbal traps, hoping He'd fall in. In one of them, an expert in the law asked Him, "Teacher, which is the greatest commandment in the Law?"

They probably hoped He would go off on some tangent so that they could discredit Him, but He replied, "'Love the Lord your God with all your heart and with all your soul and with all your mind.' This is the first and greatest commandment. And the second is like it: 'Love your neighbor as yourself.' All the Law and the Prophets hang on these two commandments" (Matthew 22:35-40). Jesus' response is what gives this book the title, The Most Valuable Catch.

You will feel the wind in your face and the rolling of the seas as we head to experience some of the thrills and adventures of commercial fishing on the high seas of Alaska. But the truth is, there is no greater adventure and no more valuable catch than to discover Jesus in all of his fullness in your life. Nothing can compare with learning to discern God's voice and experiencing the wonder of his love so deeply that you love him more than anything else in the world. Christ also challenges us to take such significant steps of faith that we live a life of legacy, sharing Christ's love, truth, and grace with our families and everyone else our lives touch. This is what it means to risk it all for what matters most.

CHAPTER 1

"DROP IT HERE!"

"Follow Me, and I will make you fishers of men."
—JESUS CHRIST, MATTHEW 4:19 (NASB)

As a young man, I was part of a five-man crew on my father's boat, fishing for halibut in the open ocean stretching across the Gulf of Alaska. I'd been fishing with him since I was ten. The work was grueling, but I loved the feel of the ocean and the challenge of being a member of a high-powered crew. (If you've watched *Deadliest Catch*, you know what I mean.) We fished twenty-four hours a day, with each of us pulling twenty-hour shifts.

On one particular trip, the weather was intense: high winds, big waves, and bone-chilling cold. We were dropping twenty miles of longline with nearly 5,000 hooks to the bottom, trying to catch big halibut. Each day, we hauled the line in, gutted, cleaned, and scraped the huge cavities of the fish, and then sent them below deck to be packed with ice. At the same time, our crew was cutting bait and preparing the hundreds of hooks for the next set. But on this trip, too many of our hooks were coming back up empty. We faced the grim possibility of not even making enough money to cover the trip expenses, which meant that even with all this work, the crew would go home empty-handed. Dad made the decision to keep the gear on board and travel for several hours to move us west of the Kodiak area. The lack of fish (and the lack of income) was at least partially offset by the desperately needed sleep we'd get on the way.

I climbed into my top bunk and packed life preservers around me so the rough seas wouldn't toss me out. I fell asleep, and God gave me a dream. I saw myself preaching in a small stadium. I didn't recognize the location, and it wasn't very big—maybe a stadium connected to a high school or a small college. I was on a stage in the center of the field. A cinder rock path separated the grandstands from the field. I was giving an invitation, and people were coming out of the stands onto the field to surrender their hearts to Christ. When I woke up, I sat up quickly and banged my head against the low beams above the bunk. I felt the jarring impact, but the dream didn't vanish. If anything, it was more real than ever. In fact, I sensed very strongly that God was communicating with me in the most intimate and profound way.

I grew up in a Christian family and knew the Lord, but thoughts of going into the ministry had never crossed my mind. In other words, the idea of me preaching—at a stadium!—had never been even a blip on my radar. Instantly, I tried to make sense of what I knew God was telling me. I prayed, "God, if You want me to change the direction of my life and go to Bible college, something has to change because I'm not making enough money on this trip to pay for it."

I sensed God's reply, Money? Is that your problem? Is that what determines if you'll follow Me? Don't worry. I can handle the money.

A few minutes later, the boat slowed down. The cook popped his head into the small stateroom and told me to hit the deck because breakfast was ready in the galley. When I sat down, I could see the rest of the crew was in a foul mood. They were sore from all the work so far, they hadn't slept well, and there were no guarantees that a change of location would put fish in the boat. But I had a feeling things were going to be different . . . really different.

Years ago, a good trip could take up to eighteen days to fill the fish hold. But that day, when we started hauling our gear, we were in the fish! It would take just a few days to fill the boat. I was absolutely sure that God was speaking to me through this fantastic turnaround. He was using it to build my faith to trust His voice.

That summer, I was on my Dad's boat for three more trips, one in Alaska and two albacore tuna trips hundreds of miles off the West Coast. By the time we tied up after the last trip, God's dramatic calling had vanished from my mind. Instead, I had my grand plans. I wanted to find an investment so I could make even more money. I found a beautiful duplex still under construction across the street from an incredible park and beach. I bought it, and on the day it was finished, I moved in with a couple of friends. On the outside, life couldn't have been better. I had a new place, great friends, and plenty of money . . . but I felt uneasy because my heart was drifting away from God and His calling. For the next couple of months, every time I went to church, it didn't matter what the pastor's message was that week. All I heard was, *Steve, what are you doing here? I called you to prepare for the ministry. Follow Me. Obey Me. Get up and get going!*

For several weeks, I tried to ignore this nagging conviction, but it was too persistent, too strong, and too undeniable. At church one Sunday, I asked God to show me one more time that He was calling me into ministry. I promised that if He would clearly show me, I would follow. When I got home, one of my roommates (who wasn't a believer) met me in the driveway. When I opened the car door, he said, "When you went out the door this morning, something woke me up. I've been thinking all this time about what you should do with your future."

His comment knocked me off guard. Who was he to tell me what to do with my life? I smarted off to him, "Oh yeah! Mike, what do you think I should do with my life?"

He didn't miss a beat. "You should be a preacher!"

I blurted out, "Why in the world did you say that?"

He shook his head and answered, "That's all I've been able to think about since you walked out the door this morning. I tried everything to shake it from my mind, but it wouldn't leave. I even cut the grass to get my mind off it, but the thought is still there. I guess there's something there for you."

Now I knew how Balaam felt when his donkey rebuked him! I was stunned. Without saying anything to my roommate, I went inside, walked upstairs to my room and got on my knees to ask God to forgive me for my stubborn, rebellious heart.

The next morning, I enrolled in a Bible college. I didn't know anyone, but it didn't matter—I was there to prepare to be what God had called me to be.

HOW GOD SPEAKS

Fishing for halibut across the Gulf of Alaska and tuna up and down the West Coast from Washington to California is a thrill and a challenge. Boat captains feel a lot of pressure to find fish in the vast expanse of the ocean. Sometimes people would ask my Dad why he went out 1,000 miles or more to chase tuna. His answer involves both art and science. Over many years in the fishing business, Dad gained a wealth of knowledge about the warm deep blue waters known as the Japanese Currents, the sea temperature the tuna prefers, the signs of birds, and other indicators. But Dad also developed his intuition, a sixth sense that was just as important as the charts. Some captains, especially those new to the job, can be indecisive, but Dad seldom second-guessed himself. With his powerful blend of years of knowledge and finely tuned intuition, he took us to his favorite halibut spots marked in his mind and his charts. He would position us and then call out to the crew, "Let's go! Drop it here! Let's blow the gear out!" Instantly, we launched a 50-pound anchor to start setting the gear. Next went the buoy bag and the radar reflector pole, and then the miles of line with baited hooks, which sank to the bottom in search of halibut. As the set was complete, another anchor was launched. The buoys and radar pole marked the end, where we would return later to haul in the lines. Was Dad right? Almost always.

At the moment of decision, Dad felt a clear prompt to drop the line. The complex factors that played into his decision are much the same as those that determine ours as we follow Christ—both art and science, intuition and past experiences, impressions from the Holy Spirit, and hard data. Sometimes we pay attention to God's prompts, but sometimes we don't. Let me explain . . .

A prompt is something that moves a person to speak or act. At the beginning of my adventure with God, He used a dream to prompt me, but I resisted. It wasn't until He spoke through my roommate that the message sank in. That's when I spoke words of commitment to the vision God was giving me; that's when I took action; that's when I moved into the jet stream of God's presence, power, and purpose.

Prompts are the hooks that keep us connected to the heart of God. They may be dramatic, but far more often, God whispers to our hearts to speak up, be quiet, give up, or give ourselves to those in need.

I don't want you to get the idea that I always get dramatic dreams. Actually, this was a once-in-a-lifetime experience (so far, at least). Similarly, we marvel at the story of God showing up to Moses at the burning bush, but as far as I know, that's the only instance in all of recorded history of a burning bush that wasn't consumed. It's entirely appropriate to ask, "Does God communicate with us? And if He does, what does it look like?" Glad you asked . . . The answer to the first question is an emphatic "yes!" The answer to the second is much more nuanced. Let me list quite a few ways God communicates with us:

THE SCRIPTURES

The Bible is the best and most powerful divine loudspeaker we can find. Through it, God speaks in every passage. In fact, Jesus is called "the Word" in John's prologue; it's His very nature to communicate with us. Paul reminded Timothy, "All Scripture is God-breathed and is useful for teaching, rebuking, correcting and training in righteousness, so that the servant of God may be thoroughly equipped for every good work" (2 Timothy 3:16-17). If you want to know God, feast on the Scriptures. If you want God to lead you, meditate on His Word. If you want God to use you, develop the beautiful blend of courage and humility as you experience His presence, grace, and purpose through every passage in the Bible.

"When God speaks, he does not give new revelation about himself that contradicts what he has already revealed in Scripture. Rather, God speaks to give application of his Word to the specific circumstances in your life. When God speaks to you, he is not writing a new book of Scripture; rather, he is applying to your life what he has already said in his Word." [1]

—Henry Blackaby and Richard Blackaby

WORSHIP

Praise and thanksgiving form a gateway to our hearts. As we take time to reflect, open our hearts, and seek God, we become more open to His voice. Revivals and times of personal refreshment are often found when our hearts are hungry for more of God, and we seek His presence and touch. Worship includes dedicated times of prayer, perhaps fasting, and maybe a retreat away from our busy schedules and all the distractions. In these times, we seek God for direction and renewal, and we can be sure that God is always responsive to a seeking heart.

---

1 Henry Blackaby and Richard Blackaby, *Hearing God's Voice* (United States: B&H Publishing Group, 2002), 18.

> Prompts are the hooks that keep us connected to the heart of God.

DREAMS AND VISIONS

Many of us read about God giving Joseph dreams in Genesis or Paul's vision to go to Macedonia and think, *That's what I'm talking about! I want that kind of divine intervention! Sign me up!* Yes, God certainly gives people supernatural dreams and specific visions. These are powerful but somewhat rare. We shouldn't count on this means of connecting with God every time we need some direction.

IMPRESSIONS

The Holy Spirit indwells every believer, and if we pay attention, we may sense a nudge forward or a "check in our spirit" to stop and go a different direction. When we feel the nudge to be generous, kind, and thoughtful, it's usually a clear sign that the Holy Spirit is at work in us, so we can confidently take action. We can fine-tune our sensitivity to the impressions the Spirit gives us, but only by obeying. To be sure, sometimes we'll be wrong, but that's okay. It's better to be sensitive and obedient than skeptical and obstinate.

WISE, MATURE PEOPLE

One of the most common ways God speaks to us is through other believers who have walked with God for a long time and have cultivated godly wisdom. They help us interpret circumstances so we can respond in bold faith, and they encourage us every step of the way. But again, they're not infallible. Look for people with a good track record who have also developed the humility that comes from knowing their limitations. If someone insists that you do what they tell you God wants you to do, be very wary. The Holy Spirit speaks words of affirmation and confirmation, and He will never contradict the Word of God.

NATURE

The intricacy of atoms and the vast expanse of the universe, the exquisite beauty of a flower and the roaring of a tidal wave … everywhere we look in nature, we see evidence of the creativity and incredible power of God. The stars speak to us of His majesty, and the things we see through a microscope tell us that God is intimately involved in every aspect of life. We can trust Him.

CIRCUMSTANCES

Sometimes, we see an answer to prayer when God opens a door of opportunity, or the answer is "no" or "wait" when a door remains closed. Every open door, though, isn't a sure sign of God's direction. We may have several good options, so we need to continue asking God for guidance. God uses blessings to tell us more about His love and generosity, and He redeems suffering to remind us that He is sufficient, no matter what comes our way. Far too often, we absorb the wrong messages from blessings and heartaches: We forget God as we enjoy what He has given us, or we assume all the good gifts come from our talents. And we blame God when we suffer, angry at Him for not protecting us. It's perfectly good and right to pour our hearts out to Him, in praise or complaint, but behind it all, a gracious God is communicating His heart to us.

PAST EXPERIENCES

As a parent, I learned (sometimes the hard way) what motivates each of my children, and I worked to tailor my communication to bring out the best in them. Together we soon developed patterns of give and take that worked, at least most of the time. In the same way, God reminds us of past experiences when He nudged us, whispered to us, or jolted us when we were off course. As we look back, many of us can see a pattern of God's involvement, so we learn to anticipate the pattern being replicated again. For me, the pattern of God's prompting usually includes insights from the Scriptures, a fresh idea of what God might do in a current situation, and the confirmation of godly friends.

The question isn't "Is God speaking?" He is, that's His nature, like a loving parent who longs to connect with their children. We don't have to beg Him, and we don't need to twist His arm. A better question is: "Are you listening?" I love the passage in 1 Samuel 3:1–10 when the boy heard the voice of God and thought it was Eli's. He went to the old man twice and said, "Here I am; you called me." When it happened the third time, Eli realized God was speaking to the boy, so he told him, "Go and lie down, and if he calls you, say, 'Speak, LORD, for your servant is listening.'" Samuel went back to bed, and he heard, "Samuel! Samuel!" And Samuel responded, "Speak, for your servant is listening" (v.10). In Hebrew, words are emphasized by doubling. For instance, when David's son Absalom was killed, David cried out, "Absalom,

Absalom! My son, my son!" Here, years earlier, God speaks Samuel's name in a way that is bold and clear. Samuel had to hear God's voice three times before he realized it was actually God speaking to him, but when he did, God gave him a special mission.

Fast forward a millennium to read Luke's account of the early church in Acts. On page after page, we see God intervening to prompt people to go in this direction or that. For instance, the story begins when the disciples are with the resurrected Jesus. Just before His ascension, Jesus gave them (and us) marching orders: "But you will receive power when the Holy Spirit comes on you; and you will be my witnesses in Jerusalem, and in all Judea and Samaria, and to the ends of the earth" (Acts 1:8). After Jesus ascended, the very next scene is quite different. Jesus could have told them whom He had chosen to replace Judas, but He didn't. Instead, they put two men forward. They didn't vote; they cast lots. That's how Matthias was added to the eleven apostles. Most would agree that the coming of the Holy Spirit at Pentecost was the day the church began. For the rest of Luke's history, we read how God led His people, sometimes with dramatic visions or remarkable circumstances, but often with an inner nudge. We might say that the Book of Acts could be titled the Book of Prompts!

It's possible to develop a sensitivity to God's heart and voice similar to your relationship with your spouse or closest friend. At the beginning of the relationship, you were just getting to know each other, and you had to spend time understanding the meaning behind the person's words. As the relationship progressed, you learned to "read" each other, anticipate responses, and in the most positive way, take each other for granted. Even then, misunderstandings happen, and they must be addressed, but you enjoy connecting on every conceivable issue that's important to one or both of you. Intimacy (or at least comfortable give-and-take) becomes normal. That's the kind of connection we can have with God.

THE DREAM UNFOLDS

I want to return to my dream as we fished offshore of Alaska. It was indeed the beginning of God's call upon my life. The journey has been more than I could have ever imagined, from great victories to days of extreme challenge and pain. I met my wife, Cheryl, in college, and we chased the dreams of God together and raised our family. Today we pastor a fantastic church family called Eastridge Church, a multi-site church with locations in Issaquah and West Seattle, Washington, and an international campus in Addis Ababa, Ethiopia.

The dream was about me preaching at a small stadium, like one next to a high school. But God had even bigger ideas: Several years ago, I had the honor to preach at a citywide evangelistic event in Safeco Field (today, T Mobile Park), the home of the Seattle Mariners. It's often described as one of the most beautiful stadiums in Major League Baseball. It even has a retractable roof. When I came to the altar call, I invited people to come forward to receive Christ so we could pray for and with them. Hundreds of people began streaming out of the stands toward the stage, where I stood over second base.

〜〜〜〜〜〜〜〜〜〜〜〜〜〜〜〜〜〜〜〜〜〜〜〜〜〜〜〜〜〜〜〜〜〜〜〜〜

It's possible to develop a sensitivity to God's heart and voice similar to your relationship with your spouse or closest friend.

At this moment, the Holy Spirit grabbed my attention, *Look at this!* I stopped and took in the incredible scene. It was what I had seen in my dream in Alaska, but way bigger. Jesus never said, "Follow Me, and you will preach in Major League stadiums." He just said, "Follow Me." At that moment, I stood in quiet awe, watching what God was doing in these people. In my heart, I was marveling at God's goodness as I thought of the end of Paul's prayer in Ephesians 3: "Now to him who is able to do immeasurably more than all we ask or imagine, according to his power that is at work within us, to him be glory in the church and in Christ Jesus throughout all generations, forever and ever! Amen" (Ephesians 3:20-21).

"Listening gives us the courage to abandon where we thought our journey would take us and trust that God is unfolding something far greater than we could imagine or bring about on our own."[2]
—Gail Johnsen

---

2 Gail Johnsen, *All There: How Attentiveness Shapes Authentic Leadership* (United States: N.p., 2020), 69.

A TURNING POINT

Doug Chase has been a real estate and construction manager for several Fortune 500 companies. One Sunday, he visited our church, and that morning's message was about Nehemiah's leadership in rebuilding the walls of Jerusalem after the Babylonian armies had destroyed them. The Word of God touched Doug that morning, and he saw himself through a different set of lenses. Like Nehemiah, his God-given talent is in overseeing large construction projects, but his heart shifted, and he now wanted to build for God's kingdom. He prayed and asked God for an open door, and before too long, he changed jobs, entered the ministry, and found his true calling. If you met Doug on the street and asked him to tell you about himself, he'd say, "God has called me to be a Nehemiah. I'm a builder for the kingdom of God." Doug took a role with the Assemblies of God to coordinate the construction of churches, and later, he came back to our church. He came at a divinely appointed time because we were in a very difficult situation in constructing our new facilities and desperately needed his help. Today, Doug is our business director, a highly valued team member, and a trusted friend. He's where God called him to be.

When he heard a sermon about Nehemiah, the Spirit of God gave Doug a new perspective on his skills, experiences, and purpose. That day's sermon was God's prompt to connect Doug with a new mission.

I want to encourage you to journey with me. Grab your duffle bag, and let's go! We're going to focus on what God has for you. Business leaders, university students, pastors and ministry leaders, moms and Dads, teenagers, and everyone else, know this: God is speaking to you about the dreams He has for you. Trust the prompt and join me—you'll feel the spray from the bow on your face and learn how to trust the Holy Spirit's prompts in your life and grow in confidence and anointing.

LEARNING TO LISTEN

Learning to listen to God's prompts and whispers is an acquired skill. It's not based on our personality or temperament. The people in the Scriptures who were sensitive to God's Spirit were bold risk-takers like Elijah and Paul and reflective people like Jeremiah and Nicodemus. In other words, everyone is admitted to the school of intimacy with God. Let me offer some lessons I've learned:

Every time you open the Bible, pray like Samuel, "Speak, Lord, your servant is listening." This simple practice reminds you that Bible study isn't like reading online news or a social media post; it's positioning yourself to pay attention to the Word—because God speaks most clearly through the Scriptures.

We should expect God's presence and power in a special way when we gather as the family of God. In fact, we should anticipate Him speaking through what has been called "the miracle of preaching." Doug Chase is far from the only one transformed by hearing God's Word preached. It happens all the time, and it's not an accident. Pastors spend hours studying and praying to sharpen their messages, and leaders in the church pray that God would anoint the pastor with supernatural power. They also pray that the Spirit would awaken hearts, convict people of sin, assure them of God's love and forgiveness, give them a new direction, and empower them to follow Jesus with all their hearts. The "miracle" that happens in the hearts of people throughout the congregations is a direct result of God using yielded servants who trust Him to change lives through their praying and preaching.

TAKE TIME TO BE QUIET

When we have our devotions, we're often rushed. We're thinking about the next thing we need to do, and we want to finish the passage we've been reading. Quite often, the thing that's crowded out is time to be quiet so we can listen to "the still, small voice" of God (1 Kings 19:12 ASV). Make quiet a priority. Even if you don't finish everything you planned to read or write, make sure you have time to listen. Missionary and author Andrew Murray wrote, "Prayer is not monologue but dialogue; God's voice is its most essential part. Listening to God's voice is the secret of assurance that He will listen to mine."[3]

We're not in a contest with other believers.
Each one of us is uniquely called to
fulfill God's purpose in the world.

OBEY THE PROMPTS

In his book Immediate Obedience, Pastor Rod Loy observes that "Jesus' attitude was a predetermined commitment to obey

---

3 Andrew Murray, *Essential Works of Andrew Murray* (Uhrichsville, Ohio: Barbour Publishing, 2008), Lesson 22.

the Father's will no matter what He said to do or where He said to go. . . . God is waiting for ordinary people to sign up for the adventure of a lifetime: to know Him more intimately, hear Him more clearly, and step out to do whatever He directs."[4] If we aren't sensing God's prompts, the problem might be that we've said "no" or "not now" so many times that our hearts have become numb to the leading of God. Obedience in one instance makes us more aware of God in the next.

There are times, though, when it seems God has vanished. Human relationships are sometimes mysterious: we misunderstand and are misunderstood; expectations aren't met; communication breaks down. As we try to relate to an infinite God who is unlike us in so many ways, we can expect confusion (but only on our end). It's inevitable, so we need insight into how to respond. The Psalms are full of honest expressions of despair as the writers wonder why God seems absent. In Psalm 42, for instance, the writer compares his spiritual condition to a deer dying of thirst. He longs to sense the presence and love of God, but the heavens are silent. Most of the psalm is, in fact, a complaint that God "hasn't shown up" in spite of his pleas, but at the end, he tells himself, "Hope in God; for I will yet praise him, my Savior and my God" (Psalm 42:11). From time to time, even the most devoted and devout among us experience God's silence. We can be sure, though, that God is present, and He's undoubtedly orchestrating events behind the scenes for our good and His glory, even when we don't see any sign of it. The famous nineteenth-century English pastor Charles Spurgeon is reported

---

4 Rod Loy, *Immediate Obedience* (Springfield, Missouri: Influence Resources, 2014), pp. 42, 44.

to have said, "God is too wise to be mistaken. God is too good to be unkind. And when you can't trace His hand, you can always trust His heart."

Don't compare or compete with how God prompts others. We're not in a contest with other believers. Each one of us is uniquely called to fulfill God's purpose in the world. God prompts us to say "yes" to an opportunity to serve, to speak words of hope to a neighbor who is struggling, to stop to pay attention to a child, to give more generously than ever, or a thousand other responses to His nudges and whispers. When we fished, we used different hooks depending on the fish we wanted to catch. God uses prompts designed specifically for each of us, so we'll stay connected to His heart.

Sometimes, you feel like God has singled you out. I've often heard people say that when I gave an altar call at the end of a service, they felt like they were the only people in the room. God was speaking to them, calling them clearly to respond in faith. Sometimes it was to trust in Christ as Savior and Lord; sometimes, to repent of recurring sin; and sometimes, to step out in obedience to follow God's leading.

"There will be no peace in any soul until it is willing to obey the voice of God." [5]
— Dwight L. Moody.

---

5 Dwight L Moody, *Short Talks* (Moody Publishers, 1900), 31.

The fulfillment of my Alaskan dream, preaching in Safeco Field.

CHAPTER 2
GRAB YOUR GEAR

"True faith means holding nothing back. It means putting every hope in God's fidelity to His promises."[6]
—FRANCIS CHAN

My preparation for fishing on the high seas started when I was young, when my Dad sometimes took me for short trips on inside waters. When I was eight, he asked me to join him in taking his boat from Anacortes, Washington, to Seattle to sell it. He planned to buy a bigger boat. It was just my Dad, one of his friends, and me.

As they were drinking coffee, I asked if one of them would pour me a cup. My Dad smiled and said, "Well, I guess if you're old enough to be on the boat, you're old enough to drink some of our coffee." He poured me a cup. When I stared down at it, it looked as thick and black as tar. I took a sip. Surely, I thought, the next one would be better. I took another sip. It wasn't. I wondered why in the world anyone would drink this stuff. It was my last taste

6 Francis Chan and Preston Sprinkle, *The Francis Chan Collection: Crazy Love, Forgotten God, Erasing Hell, and Multiply* (David C Cook, 2014), p. 120.

of coffee for decades until I became a pastor in the Seattle area, and people kept asking, "Can we get together for a cup of coffee?"

I have another coffee story that gives you a glimpse of life on a fishing boat. I was on a trip in Alaska with my Dad, and one day we were tied up to a dock. We knew the men on the boat tied next to us, and they invited us to join them. We all sat at the galley table, and the captain asked my Dad if he wanted a cup of coffee. Dad said, "Sure, thanks." The man picked up a coffee mug from the counter. He looked inside and saw coffee grounds and residue. Without missing a beat, he reached down to the floor, picked up a dirty wool sock, and wiped the inside of the cup. Then he poured it full of coffee and handed it to my Dad. I sometimes tell this story when I'm speaking on the importance of marriage, and I conclude, "It's not good for man to be alone!"

Each fishing season begins with the captain and crew pulling the gear out of the storage lockers and taking stock of everything stored from the previous season. They repair or replace equipment to ensure everything works perfectly: the line, hooks, buoys, anchors, engine, radar reflectors, and everything else. The gear that brought success last year may not be adequate to bring success in the next season. It's also important to pull the boat out of the water and dry dock it to inspect the hull, scrape off the barnacles, and clean it thoroughly. Nothing is taken for granted. The longer and more dangerous the trip, the more attention needs to be given to preparation. You don't want to be a thousand miles out in heavy seas and realize you neglected the most important aspect of life and safety when you didn't replace a critical piece of gear!

In every endeavor—family relationships, businesses, non-profits, and churches—it's crucial to prepare for the next season.

A little investment of attention and updated resources now pre-vents a world of problems later.

Even as a young boy, I wanted to be on the water with my Dad. He was a quintessential skipper of an Alaskan fishing boat—determined, calm under pressure, and with a sixth sense for where we'd find fish. At first, I went with him on the protected waters of Puget Sound, but even then, my mom was worried about me. She thought I was too young to be on a sixty-two-foot boat. When I was ten, my parents had some long conversations about Dad taking me for an extended trip on the open ocean. He finally convinced her when he said, "I'm not taking him so he'll be in danger. I'm taking him because I love him, and I want him to have these experiences with me." Then he assured her, "The first trip is just a trial run for Steve. If we realize it's too much too soon, we can scale things back."

I can't explain the rush of excitement I felt when I put on my rain slickers and stood on the side of the boat as we left the harbor of Newport, Oregon. I was part of my Dad's crew and headed out on my first real fishing trip.

The trip, though, didn't go as planned. After only a few days, a mechanical failure forced us to return to Newport for repairs. Dad was down in the engine room troubleshooting, and I was on deck bored out of my mind. I noticed a deck bucket we used to wash the deck. The bucket had a rope tied to it, and I had an idea. I threw it overboard to scare some seagulls that were close to the boat. I enjoyed the game . . . a lot more than the birds did. After a while, Dad came up to see how I was doing. He warned me not to throw the bucket in the water because if it filled with too much water, I wouldn't be able to bring it back up. I returned to my mind-numbing boredom of just sitting on the deck, but then I thought, *I'll be sure to bring the bucket up. There won't be any problem. I'm sure of it.* After a few more tosses to splash the gulls, I threw the bucket, and it filled with water. As it sank, the rope slipped through my hands until I was at the end of it. Instantly, I realized it was either me or the bucket, so I let go. I watched the bucket sink to the bottom of the bay.

A few minutes later, Dad came up from the engine room and said, "Steve, I need the deck bucket."

I swallowed hard and had to admit, "I'm afraid it's gone. I lost it overboard. I'm sorry."

Dad didn't yell or remind me that he'd warned me. He told me to go inside and look at the daily catch log and then tell him how many fish we'd caught. When I came back, I told him the number. My share was ten cents a fish. Dad pulled out his wallet and paid me my first crew share, and then he said, "There's a supply store at the top of the dock. You can buy a new bucket there." My first crew share paid for a piece of gear I'd lost. I learned my lesson: It was the only piece of gear I ever lost on a fishing trip. From the beginning, Dad taught me the importance of preparing and preserving all our gear.

PREPARING FOR MORE

God has a season of preparation for each of us. It begins with checking under the waterline of our lives. His greatest work isn't on the surface but in our hearts. This is where He prepares us by prompting, convicting, and working deeply in us. The heart is the most neglected and vulnerable area of our lives, but it is the key to everything that God can do through us.

People tend to make one of two mistakes when they sense God's prompting. On one end of the spectrum, a few people mistakenly believe they now have something over others—they're special and want everybody to know it! They need a large dose of humility so they depend on God, not themselves, to understand how to respond wisely and graciously. But many others are on the other end. They're suspicious (of their ability to discern God's leading and of God's willingness to share His heart), and they find all kinds of ways to explain away the nudge, delay their response, or deny it altogether. They're in good company. Jeremiah was one of them.

The opening chapter of Jeremiah provides incredible insight into how God speaks to us, and if we listen, it builds our confidence to trust His prompts and take bold steps of obedience. In the opening scene of Jeremiah's encounter with God, he reports: "The word of the Lord came to me, saying, "Before I formed you in the womb I knew you, before you were born I set you apart; I appointed you as a prophet to the nations" (Jeremiah 1:4-5).

When employers look at the background of prospective employees, they go back to their education and early work experience. The background check for Jeremiah began at the time before he was born: He was hired to represent God when he was in his mother's womb! How would you respond to such a dramatic pronouncement? Jeremiah told God, "Alas, Sovereign Lord, I do not know how to speak; I am too young" (v.6). It's fascinating: Jeremiah acknowledged that God is supreme, sovereign over the affairs of individuals and nations, but he said in effect, "But You got this one wrong!" He simply couldn't imagine filling the role of a prophet, a seer, to pronounce God's judgment to kings.

The Most Valuable Catch

The heart is the most neglected and vulnerable area of our lives, but it is the key to everything that God can do through us.

God didn't blink. He told Jeremiah, "Do not say, 'I am too young.' You must go to everyone I send you to and say whatever I command you. Do not be afraid of them, for I am with you and will rescue you" (vv7-8). It's like God was saying, "You acknowledge that I'm sovereign, and you're right. Now be what I'm calling you to be and do what I'm calling you to do. You won't be alone. I'll be with you every step of the way."

Sometimes, the Lord gives us a tactile experience to confirm His leading. Jeremiah tells us, "Then the LORD reached out his hand and touched my mouth and said to me, 'I have put my words in your mouth. See, today I appoint you over nations and kingdoms to uproot and tear down, to destroy and overthrow, to build and to plant'" (vv.9-10). His message to the most powerful leaders would include both judgment and the promise of blessing.

To continue the confirmation, God asked Jeremiah, "What do you see?"

He answered, "I see the branch of an almond tree." The almond tree is one of the first to blossom in the spring. I can imagine Jeremiah thinking, *Nothing big, just an almond branch. Could that even be right? Should I even speak it to God?* Have you felt that way in your life when God spoke to you and it seemed, well, confusing?

God responded, "You have seen correctly, for I am watching to see that my word is fulfilled." The branch was assurance that

God's word would come true. But God wasn't finished. He asked again, "What do you see?"

This time, Jeremiah had a different vision: "I see a pot that is boiling. It is tilting toward us from the north" (vv.11-13). God sent Jeremiah to speak to the nation in a very difficult time. Babylon would eventually come from the north to destroy Judah, but first, the invaders would hear God's judgment from the mouth of this reluctant prophet. God spelled out his role:

Get yourself ready! Stand up and say to them whatever I command you. Do not be terrified by them, or I will terrify you before them. Today I have made you a fortified city, an iron pillar and a bronze wall to stand against the whole land—against the kings of Judah, its officials, its priests and the people of the land. They will fight against you but will not overcome you, for I am with you and will rescue you."—vv.17–19

Can you relate to Jeremiah? You're not the only one who struggles with questions about hearing from God. We wonder, *Does He speak to me? Is that really God, or am I just imagining things? Can I trust my own judgment in the process?* But this is how God has always worked in His people. We find examples throughout the Scriptures, as well as in the stories of men and women like us.

Does this account of God calling Jeremiah thrill you or terrify you? I believe our Sovereign Lord has called each of us to represent Him to our fallen and broken world, those under our roofs, and those on the other side of the planet. We may be just as reluctant as Jeremiah, but we have the same assurance that the God who calls us will equip us and be with us. No, our calling probably won't be as dramatic or as historic as Jeremiah's, but we can be confident that God will whisper His leading and nudge us toward people who need to know His love, grace, power, and purpose. That's our calling ... and that's the highest privilege life can offer. Don't miss it.

"Hard work will do almost everything; but in God's service, it must not only be hard work, but hot work. The heart must be on fire."[7]
—Charles Spurgeon

DEVELOPING CONFIDENCE

We're living in a generation that lacks confidence. Researchers tell us that the number one question that Gen Z is asking is at the most basic level: "Why am I here?" As we have drifted away from our spiritual mooring as a nation (according to Barna Research, only 4% of Gen Z hold a biblical worldview[8]), it has left us with an elusive search for meaning and security in a world adrift in insecurity and conflict.

I have a great sense of urgency in my heart. I believe God is in the process of stirring something powerful in His church. In many ways, it looks like a very dark time, but actually, we're seeing signs that point us back to the challenges the early church faced—when God used ordinary believers to turn the world upside down. Great revivals have all come with just a few people sensing God calling them to respond in faith and humility, to be honest about sin and drift, and to repent and seek His grace.

7 Charles Spurgeon, *Sermons on Proverbs - Christian Classics Ethereal Library* (United States: Christian Classics Ethereal Library) https://ccel.org/ccel/spurgeon/proverbs/proverbs.xxix. html?queryID=23853936&resultID=176821
8 Jonathan Morrow. "Only 4 percent of Gen Z have a biblical worldview." *Impact 360 Institute*. Last modified May 26, 2020. https://www.impact360institute.org/articles/4-percent-gen-z-biblical-worldview/.

As I write this today, there are reports of students gathering at universities worldwide for days of worship without ceasing. Is this the awakening we've longed for? In different parts of the country, churches are experiencing times of renewal. The early church teaches us that a prompt of the Holy Spirit can start amazing things.

"The Way" was a fledgling movement, and from the outside, it looked like it could dissolve pretty easily. The decisions made in that season had far-reaching implications. Peter and John were arrested and tried by the Jewish council for healing a crippled man in the name of Jesus. They were ordered to stop talking about Jesus, but they refused. They replied, "Which is right in God's eyes: to listen to you or to [Jesus]? You be the judges! As for us, we cannot help speaking about what we have seen and heard" (Acts 4:19-20). The authorities debated about what to do to stop them, but ultimately, they let the two disciples go. When Peter and John returned to the body of believers, they praised God for their release and prayed for more boldness to tell people about Jesus . . . and the building was shaken! It must have been an exciting confirmation.

Great revivals have all come with just a few people sensing God calling them to respond in faith and humility, to be honest about sin and drift, and to repent and seek His grace.

In those early days, those who had been captured by the grace of Jesus and empowered by the Holy Spirit were determined to do anything and everything for people to trust in Jesus. This wasn't a stable, stale organization; it was a powerful (if small) movement of God! One of the marks of the Spirit's presence in the lives of believers is amazing generosity. In the pagan world, people were promiscuous with their bodies but stingy with money, but the Christians were stingy with their bodies but promiscuous with their money. Luke's account tells us about a general attitude as well as the actions of a specific person:

"All the believers were one in heart and mind. No one claimed that any of their possessions was their own, but they shared everything they had. With great power the apostles continued to testify to the resurrection of the Lord Jesus. And God's grace was so powerfully at work in them all that there were no needy persons among them. For from time to time those who owned land or houses sold them, brought the money from the sales and put it at the apostles' feet, and it was distributed to anyone who had need.

Joseph, a Levite from Cyprus, whom the apostles called Barnabas (which means "son of encouragement"), sold a field he owned and brought the money and put it at the apostles' feet." —Acts 4:32–37

Why does Luke single out this man? Joseph was of the priestly tribe of Levi, and he "wasn't from around here." He had lived on the island of Cyprus in the Eastern Mediterranean. Others were being generous with their possessions, but Joseph became known for speaking life to people, bringing hope, and putting steel in their spines. His impact was so powerful that they changed his name and began calling him "Barnabas," the son of encouragement. He's the type of Christ-follower we need today. As he sensed the prompting of the Holy Spirit, he sold a piece of land and brought the proceeds to the feet of the apostles. In this move of humility and generosity, he sowed one more seed: he demonstrated confidence in the new leaders of God's church. He trusted they would steward his gift in a way that honors the Lord and builds the church.

But this was just the start of amazing spiritual leadership lessons we'll find as we study his life together. Barnabas would become the most significant influence on the life and development of the apostle Paul. If it wasn't for Barnabas following the prompts of the Holy Spirit, the story of the church—and the book we call the New Testament—might have been very different. Barnabas was generous and got involved in people's lives when others avoided them. He took risks to love and support people others didn't trust, and his impact is felt today in every corner of the globe. He was prepared to take bold risks for the sake of the gospel.

My wife, Cheryl, and I met while studying for the ministry. When we graduated, the Lord opened the door for us to serve as youth pastors in a small church in Tacoma, Washington. On the outside, it was the least of the opportunities open to us, but no other role could have prepared us more for our future in ministry. After three years, we began to sense that God was stirring us, that change was coming, and that it was time for us to step out into the evangelistic field and travel. However, there were still a lot of unanswered questions.

A friend who was a well-known evangelist encouraged us to prepare ourselves and buy a new car so we would be ready to begin traveling. That night I began to feel a lot of anxiety. As Cheryl went to bed, I told her I was going to pray for a few minutes. As I poured out my heart, the Lord began to speak to me about His plan. I felt God was giving me a download of information and a specific plan of action. A peace swept over my heart, and I slipped into bed, not realizing that my prayer time had stretched most of the night. When Cheryl woke up, I shared what God had impressed upon me—that we were to resign our position at the church. I even identified the Sunday that would be our last at the church. I told her that I was going to go fishing with my Dad for the summer and that this would give us some money to help us launch our ministry. Cheryl was surprised, but she said, "Well, I guess you need to call your Dad."

I called my Dad and told him what I felt God had spoken to me. He was really quiet as he listened, and then he told me, "Steve, I'm sorry, but I've already hired a guy who has been with me before, and there's no way I can replace him or add another guy. Tuna fishing is just a two-man crew." I hung up the phone, surprised, disappointed, and confused that what I felt so strongly just hours before in prayer had left me looking a little crazy to my wife and parents.

But as I prayed, I still sensed God saying, "You have to trust Me and still move forward." I told Cheryl about God's confirmation, and she agreed. I met our pastor to tell him the story, and we resigned. He responded that God works in mysterious ways, and he would walk with us. He said, "Prepare like you are going, and when the time comes, I just need three days' notice."

I was touched by his gracious reply and said, "Thank you!"

When the day came for my Dad to leave on his trip, Cheryl and I decided to drive the two hours and see him off at the dock. When we arrived, the engines were running, and the groceries and supplies were all in place. They were ready. As we stood as a family to hug, pray, and say our goodbyes, the crew member stepped onto the boat and walked past all of us. Five minutes later, he stepped out of the deckhouse with a duffle bag over his shoulder. He walked over to my Dad and announced, "I'm sorry to do this to you, but I can't make this trip. My wife is at the top of the dock and told me that if I get on this boat, she won't be here when I get back." He turned and walked away.

My Dad was stunned. He turned to look at me and asked, "Do you still think God wants you to go fishing with me?"

I answered, "Yes, but I have to give my pastor three days." He shut the engines down. He was willing to wait for me.

Cheryl and I went back to talk with our pastor. Our last Sunday was the date I had previously told our pastor we would be leaving. Why did the delay and the confusion happen? Maybe for many reasons, but I believe the biggest was that we would have confidence that we were hearing from God and we could trust His promptings. Cheryl and I have drawn strength from this experience through the years when we faced critical decisions under pressure.

"The willingness to obey every word from God is critical to hearing God speak."[9]
—Henry Blackaby and Richard Blackaby

---

9 Henry Blackaby and Richard Blackaby, *Hearing God's Voice* (United States: B&H Publishing Group, 2002), 53.

JAMMIN' - GAME CHANGER

I want to challenge you to believe for great things in your life. God desires to work through you regardless of your age or your career. A moment of impact can start anywhere at any time. That's what happened to Cheryl and me. God brought an open door that resulted in thousands of people coming to Christ across our country through an outreach called Jammin' Against the Darkness. Jammin' featured Christian NBA players and top Christian music artists. The story of Jammin' demonstrates that God can open doors we had no idea even existed, and when we walk through them, He uses us to point people to the hope and freedom they can find in Christ. How great is that?

People often ask me, "How did you get involved with some of the NBA's greatest players?" It really started with the prompt of the Holy Spirit to pray for a young man named David, whose dreams were crushed when he was overlooked in the NBA draft. From the time he was a small boy, he felt God had placed the dream of playing in the NBA in his heart, but the day I met him, he told me sadly, "This is where my dreams die, and I have to move on." He asked for prayer, and I agreed to pray with him. Over the next few years, we saw God work to create an amazing path to the NBA.

One day, I received a phone call asking me to lead an outreach in San Antonio, Texas, with three members of the Spurs basketball team, David Robinson, Avery Johnson, David Wood (the young player I prayed with), and Los Angeles Lakers' star, A. C. Green.

In that moment, something wonderful happened: God was leading us to do something none of us had imagined before ... rent an NBA arena, invite a whole city to come to an event, and have star players share their faith in Christ. We were really excited about the possibility, and I told the guys, "I don't know what we should call it, maybe something like 'San Antonio: Jammin' Against the Darkness'!"

Jammin' struck a chord because it represents how a powerful dunk, sometimes called a "jam," can turn the momentum of a game. I responded, "We always talk about trusting God to use your gifts to touch people and change lives. You guys just happen to be some of the greatest basketball players on the planet, and God could use you to impact the entire city." Instantly, a vision began to unfold. I dreamed out loud: "We can set up half court, bring out the Spurs' mascot to shoot T-shirts, and pull kids out of the crowd to shoot free throws or three-point shots for autographed shoes or jerseys. Then we can do a dramatic introduction, and you can take to the court and perform demonstrations, just like an NBA All-Star weekend: a three-point shoot-out, two-ball competition, and throwing down some dunks. Then we can transition and have you guys take a handheld microphone. From the court you can share what Christ means to you. Then I'll pull the night together with a short gospel presentation and an invitation for people to accept Christ." It seemed like a God-inspired plan!

In any movement and every relationship, trust is the glue that holds everything together.

When we held the first Jammin' event in San Antonio, the altar area was filled with hundreds of people coming to Christ. The Lord used Jammin' to challenge a whole generation of Christian athletes to stand up for Christ in their cities. For the next fourteen years, we saw the Lord turn NBA arenas like Madison Square Garden into places where people who would never go to church had an encounter with the love and grace of Jesus. It was amazing to see star players like Allan Houston, Charlie Ward, Hersey Hawkins, Luke Ridnour, David Wood, Calbert Cheaney, Andrew Lang, Michael Redd, Buck Williams, Dan Dickau, and many others stand up to lead events in their cities. I can look back at that phone call when the vision gelled and captured us, but I can also look back to an introduction years before when a young, discouraged man had the courage to ask me to pray for him because he didn't want to lose the dream God had given him. Like Barnabas a millennia before, these players took a step of faith . . . and God kept multiplying their effectiveness for the kingdom. Joseph the Levite became Barnabas, the mentor of Paul. These NBA players, some who stepped up to share their faith publicly for the first time, became major influences in their cities and the league. Barnabas trusted his leaders, the apostles, to steward the proceeds of the sale of his land. He believed they were anointed by God to use it for His glory and the good of the church. In the same way, these men trusted me with their talents and their hearts. It was a great responsibility to have the trust and partnership of so many athletes over the years. In any movement and every relationship, trust is the glue that holds everything together. With it, individuals come together to become a cohesive power; without it, they bicker and fight over even the smallest issues. Leaders are high-level stewards of heartfelt gifts.

FIRST STEPS, NEXT STEPS

You may have developed the habit of being well-prepared, or you may need to work on that part of your lifestyle. Wherever you fall on that continuum, let me make a few suggestions:

FOLLOW THE PROMPTS

As you develop sensitivity to the Spirit, you'll sense nudges and hear whispers. Don't think you're crazy! Pay attention and take a step of faith.

ASK FOR PRAYER

One of the most important (and one of the easiest) early steps is to ask someone to pray for you. This forces you to articulate what you hope God does for you, and it enlists at least one other person to support you.

INVEST IN PEOPLE

Give your heart, your time, and your attention. Yes, I know. We're busy people. We have a lot going on, and we're under a lot of stress. Far too often, we don't start the day by praying, "Lord, show me one person I can encourage today." I guarantee that this prayer will be answered! We may find it so fulfilling that we begin to notice people instead of rushing past them.

LOOK FOR PEOPLE LIKE PAUL

I believe there are people all around us who have phenomenal potential to make a difference, but they sit on the sidelines because no one puts them in the game. Barnabas noticed God's hand on Paul when others saw him only as a threat. He took a risk, and it has paid off throughout church history.

EXPECT SURPRISES

Those two words seem like an oxymoron, don't they? If you expect something, it's not usually a surprise. But in the realm of faith in our infinitely loving and powerful God, we can develop an expectation that God will do "more than we ask or think."

"Radical obedience to Christ is not easy. . . . It's not comfort, not health, not wealth, and not prosperity in this world. Radical obedience to Christ risks losing all these things. But in the end, such risk finds its reward in Christ. And he is more than enough for us."[10]
—David Platt

---

10 David Platt, *Radical: Taking Back your Faith from the American Dream* (United States: Multnomah, 2010), 181.

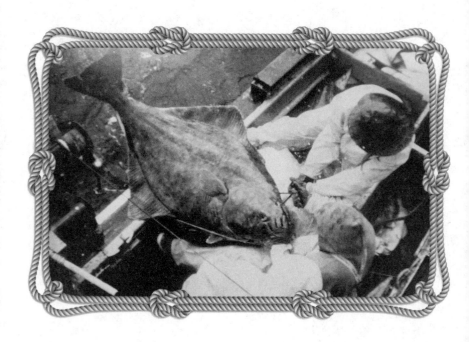

CHAPTER 3
HEAD FOR DEEPER WATER

"A ship is always safe at the shore, but that is not what it is built for."[11]
—ALBERT EINSTEIN

Yakutat Bay is an isolated outpost on the Gulf of Alaska up the coast from Juneau. There's a small Alaskan Airways runway for fishermen and hunters. Before the fishing season began, I suggested to my Dad that he hire my college buddy Tom to join our crew. He was a great guy and a good friend. We went scuba diving together, studied together in Bible college, and spent a lot of time hanging out. He was a hard worker, and the guys on the boat really liked him. Two members of our crew were retired Navy commanders, and for some strange reason, they loved pickled black cod. They kept jars of it in the galley. It was nasty stuff. If Tom began feeling a little queasy, they told him to dip into one of the jars, but Tom knew better than to even smell it. A taste of pickled black cod could make you sick if you weren't already.

---

11 John Shedd, *Salt from My Attic* (Portland, Maine: The Mosher Press, 1928), Page 20.

Tom had worked on a commercial boat seine-fishing salmon, but he was always on relatively calm and protected waters. This trip would be offshore. Tom didn't know it, but there's a world of difference between fishing on the glassy water in the bay and the rolling seas of the open ocean . . . but he was about to find out.

In late April, Dad anchored our boat in Yakutat Bay for final preparations for the trip offshore. We left home and traveled up to Ketchikan, at the far southern end of the state, and then we sailed up to Juneau before traveling on to Yakutat. At each stop, we went ashore to stretch our legs, call our girlfriends back home, and get something to eat. And we spent time at the docks preparing our gear.

At the time, the fishing season was being compressed to protect fish stocks, and the International Pacific Halibut Commission (IPHC) set an annual quota of how many pounds could be harvested each year. When I started fishing the halibut season was two trips of eighteen days each. The fishing was so good that many other boats entered the halibut fishery. The additional pressure reduced the fish stocks, so the openings were reduced year to year. On this trip with Tom, we had only twelve days. Back then, it made fishing far more dangerous because you had to fish the opening no matter how bad the weather may be. (Later, the IPHC changed the system and it has made fishing far safer).

After we got all our gear ready, it was time to fish. By this time, a storm was raging offshore. The bay waters were beginning to churn, and the sky was steel gray to the horizon. We pulled our anchor and started to head out. As Tom and I looked out at the ocean, we saw fifteen- to twenty-foot rolling waves crashing on the shore. I'd been in seas that big many times, but Tom hadn't. A few seconds later, we heard him yell so we could hear him, "Hey guys, we're not really going out there, are we?"

Dad and I and the other guys on the crew cracked up laughing. I told him, "Yeah, Tom, we really are."

Twenty-foot seas can take a toll on a person's digestion and equilibrium, but Tom fought through the seasickness and was a terrific member of our crew. I think he would agree with the seaman's adage, "The worst thing about being seasick is knowing you're *not* going to die!"

I share this story with you because it represents the challenge we will all face when God calls us to something great. Vision has to see beyond the obstacles. Proverbs 29:18 (KJV) says, "Where there is no vision, the people perish." But you need more than vision; you need faith to take action. Vision sees but faith moves. As Pat Williams states:

> *"Boldness is a form of courage, the willingness to take reasonable risks to achieve worthwhile goals. Boldness is not recklessness or throwing caution to the wind. A bold leader seizes timely opportunities, acts firmly and decisively and avoids second guessing. The confidence of the leader inspires optimism throughout the organization."* [12]

There is a time when you have to decide if you're satisfied to stay tied to the dock ... or will you take the bold step of faith to untie the boat and head to deeper waters? Are you willing to take on the risk to see God do great things in your life?

---

12 Pat Williams, *21 Great Leaders* (Shiloh Run Press, 2015), p. 21.

SEEING IN THE DARK

People sometimes have idyllic notions of what life was like in the early church. They imagine the new movement being so loving and exciting. It was, but it was also a time of severe persecution. One of the chief adversaries was a Pharisee named Saul. It seems that Saul had some kind of ax to grind. He wasn't just against the Christians; he wanted to destroy them and snuff them out completely! He made it his mission to travel from city to city to arrest and execute those who had the audacity to claim to follow Jesus.

But God had other plans. When Saul was on the road to Damascus to persecute believers there, Jesus showed up! Saul was suddenly blind and helpless, and all he had believed about Jesus was turned upside down. His companions led him into the city where he didn't eat or drink for three days. (But I'm sure he prayed!)

Two men played pivotal roles in Saul's transformation. In this book, we focus our attention on Barnabas, but in this part of the story, we find another believer who obeyed God by taking a huge risk. He was a citizen of Damascus named Ananias. As Saul sat in darkness, the Lord spoke to Ananias, "Go to the house of Judas on Straight Street and ask for a man from Tarsus named Saul, for he is praying. In a vision he has seen a man named Ananias come and place his hands on him to restore his sight" (Acts 9:11-12).

Ananias hadn't been living in a cave. He'd heard reports that Saul hated Christians, and he was on his way to his city. Of all people in the world, the one person Ananias didn't want to see was Saul! Ananias responded by reminding Jesus about Saul:

"I have heard many reports about this man and all the harm he has done to your holy people in Jerusalem. And he has come here with authority from the chief priests to arrest all who call on your name" (vv. 13-14). And he could have added, "And I'm one of them!"

The Lord reassured Ananias that the game had changed, and He had chosen Saul to share the gospel of grace with "Gentiles and their kings and to the people of Israel" (v. 15).

Ananias had every reason in the world to make excuses, to ignore the Lord's voice, and stay safe behind closed doors, but he launched out into deeper waters. He went to the house on Straight Street, where he assured Saul that, indeed, it was Jesus who had appeared to him on the road. Scales fell from Saul's eyes, his sight was restored, and he was baptized and filled with the Spirit. (I don't know who was more relieved, Saul or Ananias!)

Saul got up and entered the synagogues in Damascus. The people who listened to him were shocked. Instead of preaching against Jesus, he proclaimed Him as God's Messiah! Now, the tables were turned: Jews conspired to capture him when he left the city gates and kill him, but he escaped when some believers lowered him over the wall in a basket.

Sometimes, God is very patient in giving us plenty of clues that He wants us to trust Him for more, but at other times, the choice must be made quickly.

Saul traveled back to Jerusalem and tried to meet with the leaders of the church. Unsurprisingly, they assumed his "conversion" was a ploy to get inside their circle so he could arrest them. At this critical juncture, one man saw past the fear and realized Saul's change was genuine. Barnabas sensed the prompting of God to go to Saul. He had the courage none of the other leaders had to travel to Saul and extend him an opportunity and the benefit of the doubt. I believe this was a pivotal moment in Saul's life. Barnabas stood up for him, introduced him to the apostles, and convinced them that Saul's transformation was real.

Saul spoke boldly about Jesus, and a sect of Jews tried to kill him. The believers took him to the port of Caesarea, where he boarded a ship to his hometown of Tarsus, today a city in southern Turkey.

Of course, Saul became known as Paul, the church planter and the author of many New Testament letters to the churches. The story of the church might have been far different if Ananias and Barnabas hadn't been willing to move into deeper waters, to take a risk that Saul's transformation was real.

A CHOICE ... OR NOT

My Dad always had a carefully calculated plan when we launched the boat to go offshore. He wanted to anticipate the situation as accurately as possible, but even then, he learned to adapt to unforeseen circumstances. It happens to all of us. Sometimes, God is very patient in giving us plenty of clues that He wants us to trust Him for more, but at other times, the choice must be made quickly.

My daughter Janelle is married to an incredible young man, Brandon Kightlinger. They serve in One Voice Student Missions. When Brandon was a teenager, he was crushed when his father made the decision to walk away from their family. For years it was a place of ongoing pain as the relationship was never what he had hoped. Janelle and Brandon worked with students at inner-city schools in South-central Los Angeles, a gang and drug-infested part of the city. These schools are considered the last hope for the kids who go there. Those who know say that if these schools don't turn the students' lives around, the next institution they attend will probably be prison.

The One Voice team met with one of the principals and offered to do anything for him. He was very skeptical, so he gave them a way to prove themselves: "You can paint my office." They were glad to do it. They brought in a crew, and when they were finished, the principal was impressed. He connected them with a teacher sponsor and shortly after a Jesus Club launched reaching hundreds of students on the campus.

At another school the principal got word of One Voice and brought in their leaders to ask them what they wanted to do on his campus. He expressed that his students desperately needed positivity in their lives. Janelle and Brandon made him an offer: "We want to have a weekly student-lead Jesus Club at lunch. We want the gymnasium for the meetings. We want to bring pizza for the students."

"Done. Done. Done!" the principal replied, and then he asked, "Do you have anyone who can paint a mural?"

One Voice leaders realized someone in their community was a talented tattoo artist. "Sure," they told the principal. He told the artist he wanted a mural of people who had made a difference in history. When the artist got going, the principal walked up, surveyed the progress, and said, "What if you include Jesus? He was an important person in history."

The One Voice Team continued to find favor with this principal and watched as the doors were opened for weekly, student-led gatherings to happen at lunchtime in the school gymnasium. In one of these Jesus Club gatherings, Brandon talked about being devastated when his father chose to walk out on his family. He spoke freely and passionately to explain that it was only through his experience of the love and strength of Christ that he could overcome the hurt and forgive his father. After he spoke, a Black student approached him and said, "Hey, you said something today that I've never heard before. I never knew White Dads walked out on their families. I thought it was just Black Dads."

This young man continued to attend the weekly gathering in his high school over the next few weeks, and one day the student made a personal response to faith. He later explained, "If Jesus helped you overcome the loss and pain of your Dad leaving, that's what I needed, too." He followed the prompt of Brandon's story and the Holy Spirit's invitation, and he opened his life to Jesus. This was his way to untie and head to deeper water. It meant breaking the generational chains of his family's dysfunction and abuse. Today, he's serving God and helping many young people discover what matters most in life, the love and hope of Jesus.

But sometimes, we don't have a choice at all. We're thrown into the deep when we least expected it. That's what happened to my friend Paul Emmett.

Paul and Chris Emmett have been part of our church for years. Paul has been an executive in the financial sector, but you wouldn't know that if you saw him serve. He's very happy to play any role in advancing the kingdom. For instance, he and Chris often participated in our Jammin' events by driving our shuttle to take the athletes to the venue.

Paul is a marathoner. To stay in shape, he rode his bicycle for years from the east side of Seattle across the bridge over Lake Washington to his office, rain or shine—and a lot of days in the winter are pretty dreary in this part of the country. Tragically, a few years ago he contracted Corticobasal Degeneration, a disease much like Lou Gehrig's Disease, with progressive muscular atrophy. Today, his world has closed in around him. He is unable to travel or get around as he once enjoyed.

Still, Paul has remained a vital leader in our church. His heart and mind are sharp, he's still an elder, and he never misses a board meeting—he joins us on Zoom. As Elisabeth Elliot states, "Faith does not eliminate questions. But faith knows where to take them."[13] Paul and Chris have taught us what dignity and faith look like when facing deep waters. The same presence of Jesus that gives us the strength to untie and head toward great challenges also gives us strength and grace when we face a different form of deep water. Paul and Chris have blessed each of us as they choose gratitude and faithfulness over despair. They are a wonderful example that God can use us to demonstrate His love and glory even when we are facing difficulty or pain.

---

13 Elisabeth Elliot, *A Chance to Die: The Life and Legacy of Amy Carmichael* (Revell, 2005), Ch. 5.

DON'T BACK DOWN

Throughout the Scriptures, we find men and women being courageous in the face of daunting challenges. It wasn't that they were no longer afraid; they faced their fears and took steps forward. Moses was terrified to confront Pharaoh, and he used every excuse in the book to get out of the job. Finally, though, he chose to act, and a nation was freed from bondage. A few decades later, Joshua faced the task of forming an army out of people who were sons and daughters of slaves and had been camping in the desert for forty years. We could understand if his faith wavered, but God spoke to him:

> *"I will give you every place where you set your foot, as I promised Moses. Your territory will extend from the desert to Lebanon, and from the great river, the Euphrates—all the Hittite country—to the Mediterranean Sea in the west. No one will be able to stand against you all the days of your life. As I was with Moses, so I will be with you; I will never leave you nor forsake you. Be strong and courageous, because you will lead these people to inherit the land I swore to their ancestors to give them."*—Joshua 1:3-6

David's psalms are filled with both faith and fear, determination, and doubt. He had plenty of opportunities to wonder if he had heard God correctly when he was anointed king by Samuel, but time after time, he poured his heart out to God and received the encouragement he needed to keep trusting.

Even Jesus had to dig deep to find courage. Throughout His ministry, He told the disciples multiple times that He was going to be betrayed, falsely accused, tortured, and executed on a Roman cross. On the night before He was arrested, He went out to the

Garden of Gethsemane to spend time with the Father. Three times, He pleaded, "My Father, if it is possible, may this cup be taken from me. Yet not as I will, but as you will" (Matthew 26:39, 42, 44). Why was Jesus so shaken? Some theologians say that when Jesus was praying in the garden, He looked into the abyss of hell and realized more than ever the enormous suffering He would endure by taking the sins of every person on Himself. We get a glimpse of this terror when He tells Peter, James, and John, "My soul is overwhelmed with sorrow to the point of death. Stay here and keep watch with me" (v. 38).

Courage isn't the absence of fear; it's the presence of tenacity in the face of threats.

And yet He found the courage to face the worst in mankind, and He willingly paid the price to free us from sin and death. The writer to the Hebrews gives us insight into Jesus' motive: "And let us run with perseverance the race marked out for us, fixing our eyes on Jesus, the pioneer and perfecter of faith. For the joy set before him he endured the cross, scorning its shame, and sat down at the right hand of the throne of God. Consider him who endured such opposition from sinners, so that you will not grow weary and lose heart" (Hebrews 12:1–3). What was "the joy set before him?" It wasn't glory. He had that before He became a human. It wasn't riches. He is the Creator and owner of the entire universe. And it wasn't a close relationship with the

Father. He already had that. The one thing Jesus didn't have in heaven, and the anticipation of getting it brought Him great joy, is you, me, us. He endured excruciating suffering because He values us more than comfort. The joy of having us gave Him the courage to endure it all.

What does it take for us to head to deeper waters of faith and courage?

BE RUTHLESSLY HONEST

We want to be people of faith, but not people who hide behind their faith. Moses, Joshua, David, Jesus, Paul, and all the other leaders in the Bible had a clear-eyed view of the challenges in front of them. Accurately describing the problem doesn't make you a doubter; it prepares you to find real solutions to difficult situations.

ADMIT YOUR WEAKNESS

In The Leadership Code, the authors explain, "One of the greatest sources of stress for ambitious people is the fear of failure. Courageous and bold leaders take risks, and sometimes those risks don't work out. We have learned the simple formula for risk-taking: will to win divided by fear of failure. Increasing the will to win comes as you feel personal passion, desire to succeed, and believe in the outcome of your agenda."[14] People who are honest about their weaknesses build trust in their most important relationships ... because those people already see the chinks in their armor! I know (and I'm sure you know) people who

---

14 Dave Ulrich, Norm Smallwood, and Kate Sweetman, *The Leadership Code: Five Rules to Lead by* (Cambridge: Harvard Business Review Press, 2009), p. 140.

never admit they're wrong and never claim to have any doubts. Courage isn't the absence of fear; it's the presence of tenacity in the face of threats.

WADE INTO THE FRAY

Ask the hard questions. Find out what's really going on. And have difficult conversations, especially with people who don't like what you're doing. This is the point when many of us get defensive, which shuts down honest conversations. If this has happened before, take the initiative to say, "Sometimes, I get defensive when I hear something I don't like. If I do that again—or if I'm already doing it—please speak up. That's an area I need to grow in." Getting your hands dirty in the reality of the problem accomplishes two important goals: you will understand the situation more fully, and the people around you will feel more understood.

MAKE A DECISION

But questions, discussions, and analyses have to end at some point, and you have to choose your direction. Dad analyzed all the data and then found the point on the map where we would start fishing. Was it always the perfect choice? Of course not, but it was a lot better than sitting at the dock and never launching the boat.

WELCOME FEEDBACK

After the decision is made and steps are taken, regularly invite people to tell you how things are going. In a family, a business, or a church, we always need to make mid-course corrections, and we'll make good ones if we get input from people around us. As

Thomas Merton says, "Pride makes us artificial and humility makes us real."[15]

Avoiding risks is a sure roadblock to life's adventures, but foolish risks tell people to be wary of us. We need to develop that beautiful blend of deep security in our identity as God's chosen, forgiven, loved children, and with this firm foundation, launch into deep waters where we'll need faith and courage to tackle the challenges. The risks we take may be grand or narrow, planting a church or starting a business, volunteering for a ministry or offering a new idea for the company, or simply speaking to a new neighbor. Whatever the risk, we can be assured that God is with us, cheering us on, continuing to give us guidance, and blessing us and others every step of the way.

> *"Focus on giants—you stumble.*
> *Focus on God—giants tumble."*[16]
> —Max Lucado

---

15 Thomas Merton, *No Man is an Island* (United States: HarperOne, 1955), 119.
16 Max Lucado, *Facing Your Giants: A David and Goliath Story for Everyday People* (United States: W Publishing Group, 2006), 9.

CHAPTER 4

ALL HANDS ON DECK

"Leadership is a gift, stewarding that gift is a privileged responsibility for which we will be held accountable."[17]
—JOSEPH M. STOWELL

When you watch *Deadliest Catch*, you see the captain up in the pilot house directing the crew on the deck. Our boat wasn't the size of the huge crab boats (which require someone in the pilot house), but it was a great halibut and tuna boat, sixty-two feet long and able to hold nearly thirty tons of fish. Dad stood on the deck with the rest of us as he manned the controls, the wheel, and oversaw the hauling gear. The setup was entirely his design. He wanted to be in the thick of things. He's a hands-on leader.

His presence on the deck set the tone for the crew; we could see and feel his level of commitment to us and our success. Actually, Dad was more exposed to the weather than the rest of us. We were often in a covered area in the back called the bait shed, but he

---

17 Joseph Stowell, *Redefining Leadership: Character-Driven Habits of Effective Leaders* (United States: Zondervan, 2014), 24.

stood in the open, catching the full fury of every storm's howling wind, lashing rain, and crashing waves. Imagine this: he was not only navigating the boat from mid-ship, keeping the boat into the wind and protecting the line from the hull and propeller, but he was also using a hydraulic foot control to run the roller and allow him to gaff and land the fish. It was the most challenging job on the boat. Union captains aren't allowed to leave the pilot house, but my Dad wanted to be on deck with us.

In the summer, at the latitude where we fished, there was only a couple of hours of darkness every day. On one particular night, we'd been fishing hard for days, and we were exhausted. That stretch of darkness seemed to make things even more intense. The fish hatch was a heavy wooden rectangle in the middle of the deck. The hatch is a center of activity when fishing is good. We dress and scrape the fish on top of the hatch. On the front of the hatch, we had a station where we chopped bait. As the fish were ready, we would open the secondary lid and slide the fish below the decks to be iced and stacked.

Leaders lead, and leaders inspire, but you can't do it effectively without presence and connection.

A young, strong man named Chris was a member of the crew on that trip (actually, he had been an alternate for U.S. Olympic Cross Country Ski Team). He was a terrific worker, but on this night, he was utterly spent. We were on opposite sides of the hatch, and in the glow of the onboard lights, I could see that he was in bad shape. When you work that long and hard, back muscles can spasm, and Chris was in agony. He yelled to me to come over and hit him in the back multiple times with a rod we used to hang hooks. I hit his back over and over again, being careful not to hit his shoulder blades or spine. Chris flexed and stretched . . . and went back to work. Soon the pain was so intense that he stopped and placed his hands on the hatch to hold himself up. With his face grimacing, he said, "I'm done. I can't go on. I have nothing left."

At that moment, my Dad made a rare move: he stepped away from the controls and walked toward Chris. He quickly leaned over the hatch and looked Chris in the eye and shouted, "Chris, you're becoming a great fisherman!" And he returned to the roller without looking back.

Those words went through Chris's heart and body like a jolt of adrenaline. Dad's words of affirmation and confidence gave Chris the strength to stand back up, grab his gaffe hook, and press through. It was a breakthrough moment in the midst of the pain. Leaders lead, and leaders inspire, but you can't do it effectively without presence and connection.

THE NEED FOR HOPE

At this moment, you may feel like Chris when he was stretched across a hatch, wondering if you're going to make it through the pain you're suffering. It may be a relationship fracture, a job loss, health problems, or even a crisis in your faith. If so, you're not alone. Today, stress and depression are all around us. People have been quitting and giving up in every area of their lives.

In her book, *Wonder Woman*, Kate Harris speaks of women leaving the church at a faster rate than men. Her research shows that 72% of Christian women feel stressed, and 48% say they are overextended. She quotes a Pew Survey stating that women are choosing, "other ways" to practice their faith.[18] Barna Research found in a post-COVID poll that 42% of pastors were considering quitting the ministry because of the division and strife inside the church.[19] We have also witnessed some well-known pastors and leaders deconstructing their faith, that is, leaving the foundations of the faith for any number of reasons. At the same time, our secular culture has been trying to convince believers that our commitment to the Bible and absolute truth is archaic and should be rejected.

A SACRED TRUST

In the midst of this challenging time, God is standing alongside us with a booming voice calling for us to rise up and lead a rebirth of faith that can change both the church and our communities. Pastors and Christian business leaders across the country are sensing the Lord stirring a passion for His presence and a call to walk in a fresh anointing of His Holy Spirit. We need this level personal encounter with God to give us power, humility, and confidence to lead effectively.

---

18 Kate Harris, *Wonder Woman* (Grand Rapids: Zondervan, 2014), Infographics, p.13f.
19 "Pastors Share Top Reasons They've Considered Quitting the Ministry in the Past Year," *Barna Research*, April 27, 2022, https://www.barna.com/research/pastors-quitting-ministry/

At Eastridge we teach that spiritual leadership is a "sacred trust." I believe if we could rediscover the power of these two words, it could bring the return to authentic leadership to lead spiritual renewal and revival in our time. The concept of sacred trust is simple: ministry leadership is a gift from God to His church. Those who lead in God's name need to have the highest level of personal integrity and a sacred responsibility to love and lead well.

You need people who will watch out for your safety and won't quit on you when things get tough.

We are living in a day of opportunity as people are hungry for change, but few know how to get there. Look at what is at stake right now: The Harris survey reports that increasing numbers of women are leaving the church, but at the same time, 88% of the women stated their desire for a closer faith walk. This is just one example of the spiritual hunger that's below the waterline in our culture today.

We often talk of the church as a family, but I also see it as a crew with a purpose. There is something very special about being a part of a great crew. In Alaska, we were working in a very dangerous and challenging environment, so it's even more important to know that your crew is committed to each other and to the success of the trip, no matter what we face. You need people who will watch out for your safety and won't quit on you when things get tough. I see a powerful correlation to where the church is today. We're in a day of opportunity, but threats and challenges are all around us. This day calls for authentic leadership to step up in the church and the business world to lead with a commitment to biblical truth as the anchor to the soul, and to walk with emotional intelligence to care for people and ethical intelligence to bring integrity to lead. But as seminary president Albert Mohler states in his book *A Conviction to Lead*, our leaders must also lead with conviction: "Leaders without emotional intelligence cannot lead effectively because they cannot connect with the people they are trying to lead. Leaders lacking ethical intelligence will lead their people into a catastrophe. But leaders without convictional intelligence will fail to lead faithfully, and that is a disaster for Christian leaders."[20]

In his first letter, Peter addressed the leaders of the church scattered by persecution:

To the elders among you, I appeal as a fellow elder and a witness of Christ's sufferings who also will share in the glory to be revealed: Be shepherds of God's flock that is under your care, watching over them—not because you must, but because you are willing, as God wants you to be; not pursuing dishonest gain, but eager to serve; not lording it over those entrusted to you, but being examples to the flock. And when the Chief Shepherd appears, you will receive the crown of glory that will never fade away. —1 Peter 5:1-4

---

20 Albert Mohler, *The Conviction to Lead: 25 Principles for Leadership That Matters* (Baker Books, 2012), p. 31.

And then he leaned into those who were followers:

In the same way, you who are younger, submit yourselves to your elders. All of you, clothe yourselves with humility toward one another, because God opposes the proud but shows favor to the humble. Humble yourselves, therefore, under God's mighty hand, that he may lift you up in due time. Cast all your anxiety on him because he cares for you. —vv. 5-7

The second side of "sacred trust" is what every Christ follower needs to see as their part of being a part of God's crew: The dedication to stand with the same sense of urgency and dedication to the Lord as they expect from their leaders. God is calling for a revival in our hearts of loving God and loving His people. The church is God's most prized possession. Never allow yourself to become a critic of the church or dismissive of the importance of being a part of the body of Christ. We hear professing Christians who complain, "I am done with church! I can get what I need on a podcast while I'm at the gym."

The truth is that the church should be just as important to us as it is to Jesus. The kingdom of God centers on the church, His bride. The Lord has chosen to work through His church to change our lives and change the world. God uses His church to bring people together, to teach, comfort, and build ministry. Let me explain the value of the church with a simple example: If someone were to come to those of you who are husbands and say, "I really like you and want to develop a friendship with you, but I can't stand your wife," I can assure you that those words would quickly limit any relationship you would have with that person. So, don't think you can tear into the church, the bride Jesus loves, and still have a real relationship with Him. If you have had a bad experience in a church, don't let that keep you from the place where God will use you and sharpen you. Keep looking. God will lead you.

A healthy and powerful church is only found where the pastors and the people are equally committed to the gospel of Jesus and each other. The sacred trust is not just how your pastor should live to honor God; it's how each of us should live out our faith. Your pastors need to hear and sense your commitment and support for them. You can lift the heart and strength of your leaders by expressing your love, support, and appreciation for their conviction and leadership. They're facing attacks, and sometimes being set up by special interest groups who would like to publicly shame or embarrass them for standing on biblical truth.

It's time to dream again and envision what God wants to do today to anoint His people and build His church. The great news is that the book of Acts is His blueprint for the early church, and it's just as powerful today!

THE RIGHT PLAN AT THE RIGHT TIME

When we think about the life of the apostle Paul, we usually skip from his meeting Jesus on the Damascus Road to his missionary journeys. It's easy to overlook a turning point in the story. As we've seen, after Paul met Jesus and preached in Damascus, he returned to Jerusalem to meet with the church fathers. They were understandably suspicious, but Barnabas stepped in to validate Paul's change of heart. Paul then went away to Arabia for about three years and then home to Tarsus for what may have been ten years. In other words, Paul wasn't an integral part of the story for more than a dozen years!

During this time, the Christians in Jerusalem were persecuted, and many fled to other cities, including Antioch. At first, they spoke only to Jews about Jesus being the Messiah, but some new believers from Cyprus and Cyrene came to Antioch and preached to the Gentiles. Many of them came to faith in Jesus. When the church leaders in Jerusalem heard about the work of God in Antioch, they turned to a trusted partner to go there and lend leadership to Antioch—they sent Barnabas. Luke tells us, "When he arrived and saw what the grace of God had done, he was glad and encouraged them all to remain true to the Lord with all their hearts. He was a good man, full of the Holy Spirit and faith, and a great number of people were brought to the Lord" (Acts 11:23-24).

Up until this point, a few Gentiles had believed in Jesus, but the vast majority of believers were Jews. In fact, Christianity was considered just one more Jewish sect, not a separate faith. Now in Antioch, the complexion of the church looked much different. Who could teach this blend of Jewish and Gentile believers what it means to become one body of Christ, equal citizens in the kingdom of God? Who could address the deep animosity between Jews and Gentiles so the love of God could tear down walls and build bridges? Barnabas knew just the guy!

Barnabas hadn't seen Paul in more than a decade, but the last report was that he was living in his hometown of Tarsus, in what is now southern Turkey, about a hundred miles away from Antioch. Barnabas didn't blink. He got on the road and walked to Tarsus, hoping Paul was still there, hoping his faith in Jesus was still strong and hoping he would be willing to come back to Antioch to help the church continue to grow. Luke explains that the quest was a success: "... and when he found him, he brought him to Antioch. So for a whole year Barnabas and Paul met with the church and taught great numbers of people. The disciples were called Christians first at Antioch" (v. 26). This was shared leadership at its finest: two men, very different in skills, gifting, and temperament, but united in their passion for serving God and His church.

Barnabas was an incredible example of a Spirit-filled leader. His leadership serves as a model for pastors and Christian business leaders today. Jesus calls pastors to shepherd the people and build His church. The best pastors seek to model ministry in the footsteps of Jesus, who was a hands-on, visionary leader. Jesus had clarity about who He was and the purpose of His ministry. He taught and modeled His leadership expectations, and He instilled vision and confidence in His followers so they could find their place in ministry. The church today needs strong, Spirit-led leaders who love their people and equip them to change their world.

Barnabas exemplified this type of leadership. His humility and love for the church opened the door for a multiplying effect as he made room for Paul to use his great gifts. He was willing to share his leadership, influence, possessions, and love so the church could grow and change the world. We don't see this bold selfless leadership very often today.

I love this because it reveals another Eastridge core value: "Church first." As a leadership team, we can't afford to favor a particular ministry, but we must always pursue what's best for the church as a whole. The church has to win in every situation.

This concept is amazingly powerful for building a culture of mutual respect and unity. Love for the Lord and His church is the foundation that God can use to change the world. Consider what could happen today if we rediscover this heart and passion to release people in their God-given ministries and gifting.

> *"The role of the leader is not to come up with all the great ideas, The role of a leader is to create the environment in which great things happen."*[21]
> —Simon Sinek

The primary connection for a leader is with God, to love Him and serve Him with all his heart. The second connection is with the people being served, encouraging and equipping them to love, lead, and serve. Pastors and business leaders need to create "leadership pipelines": attracting, selecting, training, placing, and shepherding rising leaders as they assume positions of service. "Great leaders roll up their sleeves and invest in the growth of their people. This involves expressing trust in people and their decision-making abilities and equipping them with proper training to innovate and lead."[22]

My Dad couldn't run a fishing boat by himself. He had to have a skilled crew to operate the roller, bait the hooks, dress the fish, and handle the dozens of other tasks on board. In the Old Testament, we see where Moses tried to be a one-man band. He was a terrific leader, but at a particular point in his story, he desperately

---

21 Simon Sinek. *Start with Why: How Great Leaders Inspire Take Action.* (United States: Penguin, 2009), 99.
22 James Kouzes and Barry Posner, *The Leadership Challenge: How to Make Extraordinary Things Happen in Organizations* (Germany: Wiley, 2017), 243.

needed to create a leadership pipeline. It took honest advice from his father-in-law to get him in gear. When Jethro came to visit, he saw that a crowd of people pressed Moses for decisions every day. Exodus 18:14 recounts how he told Moses, "What is this you are doing for the people? Why do you alone sit as judge, while all these people stand around you from morning till evening?"

Moses complained, "Because the people come to me to seek God's will. Whenever they have a dispute, it is brought to me, and I decide between the parties and inform them of God's decrees and instructions" (v. 15).

Jethro didn't let Moses off the hook by feeling sorry for him. He gave him clear directions:

"What you are doing is not good. You and these people who come to you will only wear yourselves out. The work is too heavy for you; you cannot handle it alone. Listen now to me and I will give you some advice, and may God be with you. You must be the people's representative before God and bring their disputes to him. Teach them his decrees and instructions, and show them the way they are to live and how they are to behave. But select capable men from all the people—men who fear God, trustworthy men who hate dishonest gain—and appoint them as officials over thousands, hundreds, fifties and tens. Have them serve as judges for the people at all times, but have them bring every difficult case to you; the simple cases they can decide themselves. That will make your load lighter, because they will share it with you. If you do this and God so commands, you will be able to stand the strain, and all these people will go home satisfied."—Exodus 18:17–23

This is the first instance in the Scriptures of a leadership pipeline! Jethro's advice was, in effect: "Select capable, godly men, appoint them over segments of the community, let them serve without micromanaging, and you can handle the really tough issues." And the result? The new leaders will excel, your life will be much better, and the people will be served far more effectively—a win, win, win.

It's very interesting to see that a father-in-law was the person who spoke into Moses's life . . . and he listened. Jethro had a stake in Moses's leadership. His daughter and grandchildren were affected by Moses's exhaustion and the people's complaining. Who else would have had the platform to say, "Hey, you're killing yourself by working so hard, but it's not working for you or the people. I appreciate the effort, but you need to make some changes."

The Holy Spirit prompted Jethro to speak up. His advice was to be shrewd in selecting rising leaders and build a relationship of sacred trust with them. Moses was still the leader, but now he had a crew around him who were committed to the success of the venture. I'm quite sure they brought very different skills to the work. That's part of the beauty of the family of God—we are a kaleidoscope of talents, forming new patterns of power and beauty as the Spirit of God works in us and through us. And rising leaders have different capacities. Jethro told Moses to observe each person he selected and assign them to shepherd ten, fifty, a hundred, or a thousand people. That's our task, too. We can have the same heart of love for God, but we may have very different leadership capacities, often because we have additional pressing responsibilities of family life, but sometimes just because we're wired differently.

As a lead pastor, I work hard to build a leadership culture which engages and equips our people in areas of service that best fits their talents and bandwidth. Leadership development must be our passion. "No organization should outpace the Church in developing leaders. Why should we not be outpaced? No other gathering of people has a greater mission, a greater promise, or greater reward."[23]

Let me outline some of the most common reasons people hesitate to serve in a church:

Some are reluctant to serve because they don't feel understood. No one has taken the time to get to know what makes them tick so they can be placed where their enthusiasm and skills can flourish.

Others are afraid that if they say "yes" one time, they'll be saddled with an ever-increasing load of expectations. They feel like they're about to fall into a black hole of responsibility.

Many are asked to do a job, but they receive very little training or resources. They feel like they've "been left outside to dry."

Sometimes, leaders don't explain how each role is essential to fulfill the overall vision of the church.

Some leaders push people to perform without shepherding them with love, so people can feel used.

Still, others feel overwhelmed with the burdens of life, and they can't imagine looking beyond their own needs. Some believe they're too young; others too old.

Moses figured out how to select, equip, and lead his crew. That's the challenge of today's church leaders. The challenge of

---

23 Eric Geiger and Kevin Peck, *Designed to Lead: The Church and Leadership Development* (United States: B&H Publishing Group, 2016), 67.

followers is to be open to new possibilities, sense the Holy Spirit's directives, and jump in with both feet!

Shared leadership is a core value in the New Testament church as well. In Acts Chapter 6, exposed needs called for a new leadership model. As the body of believers in Jerusalem grew, the love of Jesus attracted a lot of people, including widows who generally were the poorest of the poor in that culture. But there was a problem: Greek-speaking widows felt overlooked because the Hebrew-speaking widows were getting more attention . . . and resources. The apostles heard the complaints, but they didn't just tell the Greek-speaking women, "Get over it! Trust God. You shouldn't complain." Instead, they appointed seven men "full of the Holy Spirit and wisdom" (Acts 6:3) and gave them the responsibility to care for the widows.

Who were these men? We get a good idea by looking at their names—they all had Greek names! Greek-speaking leaders were assigned to care for Greek-speaking widows. The apostles didn't see this as a mundane administrative job. The seven became servant leaders who also cared for the physical and spiritual needs of the widows. The apostles laid hands on the men and prayed that God would bless their work. And He did. "So the word of God spread. The number of disciples in Jerusalem increased rapidly." But that's not all. Get this: "And a large number of priests became obedient to the faith" (v. 7). This is a stunning development. The priests had a vested interest in temple worship and the status quo. They had been defiant when Jesus came to Jerusalem, but now, the grace and truth of Jesus reached even into the temple to transform the priests. It seems they connected the dots between the blood of the sacrifices and the blood sacrifice of Christ.

The sacred trust between leaders and followers applied in the first century and it applies today. It applies in house churches and megachurches. The principles of integrity, compassion, and truth aren't relegated to one kind of leader; they apply to all. And the principles of openness, willingness, and enthusiasm apply to those sitting on a sofa in a house church and to those in the farthest row in a massive auditorium.

It's important for people to see and understand how ministry works. The methods of churches and the programs will vary greatly around the world, and that's good. But there are some key principles of ministry that can work everywhere.

Our mission at Eastridge is "To bring the life-giving message of Jesus to the people of every generation, from across the street to around the world." We have created a four-step pathway for personal spiritual growth. We try to make the pathway as clear as possible with two audiences in mind: those we want to disciple and those who lead the ministries. The pathway includes:

1) Discover Jesus. We want to create the path for people to discover who Jesus really is.
2) Grow in community and find freedom. We want people to know they aren't alone; God has created us for relationships.
3) Find your purpose. We want to help you become all that God has created you to be.
4) Change your world. We're called to GO! We're designed to reach across the room, across the street, and over all barriers to bring the message of Jesus to people.

All of our ministries flow out of these four pathways. When a person walks through the door of our church we consider them to be coming on deck with us. Our desire is that they would feel at home and have all obstacles removed so they can hear the voice of God. From the first moment, our ministries are designed to make relationships the priority. When people see the pathway that best fits them for where they are in their lives, we can help them find a place they would love to serve. We've found that people grow deeper, stronger, and faster when they are serving, and it is also a direct path to many new and meaningful relationships.

The principles of sacred trust and shared leadership will produce unity and commitment in any church family. They encourage people to grow strong in their faith and tackle the obstacles all of us face from time to time. In this hothouse of growth, we develop rich, honest, encouraging relationships that sadly are rare in the broader culture. And we develop a bold faith to ask God to use us in big ways.

WHATEVER THE WEATHER

I have deep admiration for people who look for opportunities to give it everything they've got. Let me tell you about an unexpected ministry partner, as well as a couple whose faith amazes me.

When we held Jammin' events, we only scheduled them when an NBA player in that city invited us to come and committed to being part of the program. That was just the first step in a long series of things that had to happen for Jammin' to be successful. We met with pastors to enlist their involvement because we wanted to send new believers to churches where they would be nurtured in their faith. And we always needed security. Bringing thousands of young people to an arena carries some obvious risks. When we were invited to have an event in Puerto Rico, we were in a very different world, but God provided in a most unexpected way. One time when I was in Washington, D.C., I met a man who introduced himself, "I'm Andy. I'm an FBI agent stationed In Puerto Rico. If you're ever there and you need anything, I'll be glad to help."

A few months later, it was time to take him up on his offer. I called and said, "Andy, I don't know if you remember me. We met when I was speaking at your home church in D.C."

Instantly, he remarked, "Of course, I remember you! What can I do for you?"

I explained how Jammin' worked, and I asked him for advice about security at our event at the Roberto Clemente Arena, where some NBA players were going to show their skills and share their faith. I told him, "We need security for the event, and I don't know where to start."

I was surprised when Andy told me, "Steve, I want you to know that I'm just one of a mighty army that God has already prepared in advance for you. Don't worry about security. I've got it." I felt really relieved. I trusted him, but I wasn't sure what it all meant.

Our event team and the NBA players flew to San Juan before the event. As soon as we got into our vehicles, a police escort drove in front and behind us to the hotel. It looked like a presidential motorcade had shown up! I felt a little embarrassed but a lot relieved. For the rest of our time in the city, Andy orchestrated all the security we needed. He could have done all that just as an administrative service, but he saw his work as part of God's kingdom, fighting against the schemes of the enemy and making way for God to do amazing things in people's lives.

When Doug Hunt and his wife, Sheila, moved to our city from Montana, they brought their four small children. They joined our church, and when we held a season of fasting and prayer, they bought in. This was a new experience for Doug; he'd never fasted before. One day during this season, he was driving on a highway, and the Lord prompted him to pull over and pray. He sensed God wanted him to be involved in getting the gospel to more people.

A few weeks later, we launched a fundraising campaign to pay for our new building. Doug felt led to commit to give $10,000. He had no earthly means of giving that much, but that's what he felt God wanted him to pledge. Throughout the year, Doug and Shelia stretched every dollar, prayed, and sacrificed, but when the year ended, they fell short of their goal. It was devastating to Doug; he felt that he had missed God and let Him down. As he prayed, he sensed God tell him, "Don't be discouraged. Just double the pledge amount for this year." It seemed ludicrous, but he felt sure God had given him clear direction. That year, God blessed him financially, and he met his pledge. In the next year of our campaign, Doug again asked God for direction, and he sensed God leading him to double it again. Again, God blessed, and he met his pledge.

We are in an area that is very difficult to build, with many different obstacles of zoning, land availability, and environmental protection issues. After spending years in the county process and simultaneously working on the architectural design, we had our permit. Now another challenge arose: from the day the permit is given, you only have five years to complete your project, or you lose the permit. When we finally received the permit, it was like someone pulled the trigger on a starter's gun. We were off and running!

We had all kinds of all church meetings and vision events. In addition, I had an opportunity to meet with leaders of our church, and I shared the challenge to develop a new twenty-acre campus. I explained my confidence that God was going to use willing people to help meet the financial needs, and for that to happen, He would have to make a way for our people. I explained the difference our church could make in our area, and I outlined the cost projections. After the meeting, Doug walked over to me and said, "Pastor, I'm believing God to allow me to give a million dollars over the next three years."

His statement was amazing on a number of levels, knowing the faith journey God put him through the past number of years, but I didn't doubt him. I responded, "Doug, I love your heart, but before you make that commitment, I think you need to go home and have a good conversation with Sheila and make sure you're in agreement."

A few days later, I saw Doug. He told me, "Sheila and I talked about it, and we realized that if we keep doubling our pledge over the next three years, it will be a little more than a million dollars. That's our pledge, Pastor."

I replied, "Okay then, I'm going to believe God with you!"

On the day we moved into our new facility, Doug brought me a check to complete his pledge of over a million dollars. This was the guy who missed completing his first pledge. Many people would have given up at that point, but Doug didn't quit. He and Sheila listened to the prompt of God and trusted Him for great things. By responding to God's leading in their lives, God has expanded both Doug's business and his kingdom influence. When you talk to Doug about how things are going, you are going to hear how God is winning people to the kingdom and how lives are being changed.

COME ABOARD

If you're reading this book, you're almost certainly already on deck in some capacity as part of your church's crew. If not, this is a great time to look for a place where you can learn, grow, and serve. Let me offer a few ideas about how you might make an even bigger impact:

EVALUATE YOUR CURRENT ROLE

If you were an observant leader in your church, what role would you see for yourself? In other words, what's your highest and best opportunity to make an impact for Christ? Are you in that role now? What would it take for you to be prepared for that role?

MAKE SURE YOU'RE ON BOARD WITH THE PASTOR'S VISION

What are the core principles that drive the church forward? What's the engine of growth? How is the church finding the blend of personal growth and effective outreach in the community? Do you have any questions about the vision or direction of your church? If so, schedule a meeting and ask your leadership team questions from a positive and supportive stance.

BE A POSITIVE FORCE ON SOCIAL MEDIA

Lean against the negativity, sarcasm, and lies about Christ, Christians, your church, and your leaders. Before you post, think and pray. Don't just react to someone else's post. Instead, consider how you can have the most God-honoring, constructive impact.

If you have any kind of leadership role in your church, regularly take time to notice each crew member's contribution and make it your mission to appreciate, affirm, and encourage each one.

APPRECIATE THE COURAGE OF YOUR CREW

Every parent, leader, and friend needs to become an expert at giving encouragement. Some of us do it naturally, but others have to make more of an effort. To be effective, it must be genuine, regular, and specific. If people believe we don't mean the nice words coming out of our mouths, our words do more harm than good. If they rarely hear them, they'll wonder if we really care. And if all we say is something general, like "You're great!" it won't make much of a dent. We need to take a minute to think about what we're going to say, and then describe what we're appreciating, such as, "I noticed how you spoke to that person who felt lonely. You stopped what you were doing, you gave eye contact, and you spoke in a kind and considerate way. I'm sure he really appreciated your kindness. I know I appreciate it."

All of us are invited and summoned to join the crew of our local church. We may need to make some adjustments in our schedules and priorities, but only the things we do in the name of Jesus will last for eternity. If you're not yet part of the crew, jump on board. If you're on the deck, consider where you can have the biggest impact.

The truth is that the church should be as important to us as it is to Jesus.

CHAPTER 5

EARN YOUR PLACE WITH THE CREW

"When you delegate tasks, you create followers, when you delegate authority, you create leaders."[24]
—CRAIG GROESCHEL

In the Alaskan fisheries, people compete for every job. They show up from all over the country to see what it would be like to work on a boat. Most have no idea of the competition they face for the opportunity. If you get selected, you'd better be ready because there's only one chance to prove you belong on the deck. In fact, you won't even have the chance to make the same amount of money on the trip as the experienced crew members. Most "greenhorns," or first-time crew members, receive a one-half crew share (some boats start at a quarter share), and if they work hard and prove themselves, they'll get invited back to work for a three-quarter share, and eventually, they will be welcomed as a full crew member. It's a far cry from the "Disney fast pass" that many applicants expect when they seek a position.

---

24 Craig Groeschel, *How to Grow a Culture of Empowering People* (LifeChurch: Podcast video, July 20, 2022), https://finds.life.church/grow-influence-without-growing-control

The Most Valuable Catch

In our church, we often call "all hands-on deck" moments if we see a ministry area struggling or we see people in need that are being missed. Great team members quickly step up and give their best when a teammate needs help. In Jammin', our NBA players were always quick to remind us that the name on the front of the jersey is more important than the name on the back.

On a boat or in the church, when looking for a great crew, we look for important traits like character, competency, chemistry, faith, and people skills. One of our key mantras at Eastridge is: "All quality ministry flows from relationship." When people can sense our love and care, it makes all the difference.

One of our most challenging Halibut openings was only four days long. Can you imagine the pressure to make as much as you can in such a short amount of time? We decided that we would push ourselves and see if we could make it all four days without anyone stopping to sleep. We made it three days straight on deck. It took three of us to begin setting the gear. Each of us had a specific role and knots that we had to have in place before launching. Once we tied our knots, we always reached over and checked each other's knots to be sure we were ready. My Dad called out to us from the deckhouse and asked if we were ready, and we all said, "Yes."

"Cut it loose!" came the command, and we all launched, first the anchor, then the buoy and the radar flagpole. We watched as the anchor sank and everything else drifted apart. None of us had tied anything together. This was where the "keep going no matter what" experiment ended, and we shut down for four hours to sleep before someone was injured. Then we got back at it and finished the trip.

> You have gifts, talents and experience that God desires to anoint first in the service of the church and then out into your business and community.

This story speaks of how strong leaders put the health and safety of their crew first, even when it costs them personally. As a crew, we wanted to stay on deck and push nonstop all the way through for the four days. We knew that there was potentially a big financial return for each of us for maximizing every hour. As the captain, my Dad had a different perspective; he was willing to let young guys give their best shot, but at the first sign that we were making mistakes and putting ourselves and each other at risk, the operation was shut down. Our lives and safety were more important to him than striving for every last dollar.

If you serve at Eastridge, you've heard the "knot story", it's become legendary. We live this story out by placing the health of our leaders and our people as the highest value. We are a healthy church and leadership team with strong longevity, in a large part because our leaders know we value their lives and families. Leadership is demanding and often there are times that we must be willing to press through for the sake of the church. Build your teams for the long haul by creating a strong team commitment to watch out for each other. Help pick up the slack when you see someone in need, and help each other maintain healthy rhythms.

I appreciate all of the business leaders who are reading this. I want to express to you how much you're needed, not just in the corporate world, but the church. You have gifts, talents and experience that God desires to anoint first in the service of the church and then out into your business and community. Thomas Moore speaks of the value of finding your place to serve, "Finding the right work is like discovering your own soul in the world."[25]

I pastor on the eastside of Seattle and our church is filled with leaders from some of the world's largest corporations such as Microsoft, Amazon, Google, Starbucks, Costco, Boeing, T-Mobile, and many others. I find that many business leaders are hungry to serve, but sometimes are uncertain if they are needed or where to even start.

God will work in your life and bring even greater fulfilment when you see him using your talents and experience for what matters most, helping people find Christ in their lives. The key is to communicate to your leaders that you are interested in meeting them and getting involved. Look for the communication pathway of the church, such as website or class sign-up. This will start a process of bringing you on the crew of the church and learning how to best serve.

On our boat, we proved ourselves by our quick responses to situations, our clear communication to the captain and the rest of the crew, and by our sheer strength to manhandle the fish. In a church, people prove themselves by following the example of Jesus: loving the unlovely because God loved us when we were unlovely rebels and aliens, forgiving those who hurt us because Jesus forgave us beyond measure, and accepting those who are different from us

---

25 Philip Yancey, *The Jesus I Never Knew* (United States: Zondervan, 2008), 39.

because Jesus accepted us even though our selfishness and sin couldn't have been more different from His holiness.

Integrity isn't just important in the lives of pastors, staff teams, and board members. God calls each of us to earn our place on the crew. Please don't misunderstand: I'm not talking about earning our salvation. It's a grace gift that we receive; we can't earn it. But we're called to be *"as shrewd as snakes and as innocent as doves"* (Matthew 10:16). This means that trust, the glue that holds the body of Christ together, must be earned by our honesty and our commitment to the good of others. As Henry Nouwen writes, "When we are securely rooted in personal intimacy with the source of life, it will be possible to remain flexible without being relativistic, convinced without being rigid, willing to confront without being offensive, gentle and forgiving without being soft, and true witnesses without being manipulative."[26]

We could look at many passages describing the kind of lives that show we're trustworthy, but we'll focus on one. In Paul's letter to the Christians in Rome, he gave them a high standard:

Love must be sincere. Hate what is evil; cling to what is good. Be devoted to one another in love. Honor one another above yourselves. Never be lacking in zeal, but keep your spiritual fervor, serving the Lord. Be joyful in hope, patient in affliction, faithful in prayer. Share with the Lord's people who are in need. Practice hospitality. Bless those who persecute you; bless and do not curse. Rejoice with those who rejoice; mourn with those who mourn. Live in harmony with one another. Do not be proud, but be willing to associate with people of low position. Do not

---

26 Henry Nouwen, *In the name of Jesus: Reflections on Christian Leadership* (United States: Crossroad Faith & Formation, 1992), 31.

be conceited. Do not repay anyone evil for evil. Be careful to do what is right in the eyes of everyone. If it is possible, as far as it depends on you, live at peace with everyone.—Romans 12:9–18

How is your church doing in representing Christ by living according to these benchmarks of integrity? How are you doing? The people around us—in our homes, at work, in church, and in our neighborhoods—are looking to see if our faith is real. Paul's description of a genuine disciple challenges all of us . . . and it amazes those who are watching!

The business of the church is spreading the amazing love of God to everyone near and far. We're in the people business, but then, so is everyone else. Surgeons are known for being dispassionate and calculating, but the best of them move beyond knowledge and skill to genuinely care for their patients. Plumbers need to be skilled at their profession, but they serve people, not pipes. Programmers may stare at screens all day, but their work is designed to make life better for those who use their products. And in the church, every role—every leader and every volunteer on every team—exists to bring Jesus's grace and truth into the lives of those they serve.

When we examine the life of Barnabas, we see this kind of heart, this kind of authentic love for God and for people. Again and again, Luke describes how he stepped into difficult situations to speak words of affirmation. He believed in Paul when the apostles doubted the sincerity of his transformation from persecutor to preacher, he walked a hundred miles to find Paul and bring him to Antioch to shepherd the fledgling church, and he invested his time (and his life) in Paul's mission to take the gospel to places that had never heard of Jesus. But let's go back to the beginning. When we first meet Barnabas in Luke's account, his name was Joseph. When people experienced the depth and wealth of his love and generosity, they began calling him a name that fit perfectly: "son of encouragement," Barnabas. Is that how people in our churches and our communities see us? I sure hope so. Or do they see us as narrow and opinionated, more wedded to our theological or political views than to the love of God?

> *"According to Jesus, leadership is not about the position that you hold or the power you get to leverage from that position.*
> *"It's about who you are at the core and how you perceive yourself as a leader. Servanthood is a character trait. Servants know who they are, and that self-awareness determines how they act . . . how they lead. Great outcomes follow."*[27]
> —Joseph M. Stowel

People are watching us. An executive of a major tech company who has served on our board spoke up in one of our meetings about watching how I led our church and board with concern for the people had a profound impact on him. He said, "I have been here through the years, and I've seen how you deal with difficult people. You never tear into people. You always speak to them in a direct and loving way, looking for a positive way forward instead of overwhelming them with their mistakes. Watching you has changed how I interact with people on my team."

The CEO of a major Seattle-based real estate company with hundreds of agents was part of our church for a long time before

27 Joseph Stowell, *Redefining Leadership: Character-Driven Habits of Effective Leaders* (United States: Zondervan, 2014), 52.

he and his family moved to another city. It was a lot of fun to be his guest at a huge company meeting to cast vision to his people. He had a number of well-known business leaders speaking and incredible music. In the middle of it all, he leaned over to me and said, "I learned this from the vision banquets at our church. Your people work hard, and they feel valued. You make a point of creating a culture of appreciation, and it shows in the enthusiasm of every person who serves at our church."

The key to effective ministry is creating a positive, faith-filled leadership culture.

Those comments, and others like them, are answers to prayer. From the beginning, I've wanted to instill in our people that serving isn't primarily about tasks and deadlines. Everything we do is to point people to Jesus, and His love makes everything we do far more meaningful than just getting stuff checked off a list.

I'm glad for people to come to our church and attend services to check us out, but I'm convinced that the purpose and connections we all long for can only be realized when our hearts are filled with the love of God and we serve together to advance God's kingdom. Each person earns his or her place on the crew by demonstrating humility, teamwork, and passion. Leaders earn their place by treating all people—insiders and outsiders—with respect, tapping into the love of God for their motivation, and affirming people who take steps of faith, big or small.

The key to effective ministry is creating a positive, faith-filled leadership culture. People need to be challenged to grow and live kingdom-centered dreams, and leaders must be careful to build healthy teams. This includes watching out for the health of our people and their families. At our church, we place a high value on building a healthy culture where people are loved and appreciated. This is lived out within each ministry department of our church and also on a churchwide level. These leadership principles are true in church and business. You will always benefit from outstanding leadership training, times of team appreciation, and just having fun together. We have found it helps instill what Danita Bye describes as the desire to *"Develop an action mind set to be a solutions provider, not just a problem identifier."*[28]

Please don't misunderstand: Tasks need to get done, schedules are important, checklists are helpful . . . but they are means to the end of sharing the love of God and transforming lives by the power of the Spirit, not an end in themselves. When people join our team, I explain that their primary role is loving people. Everything they do is shaped by that motivation, which in some ways makes them more passionate about getting things done, but in other ways causes them to slow down and really connect with the people they lead and serve. I encourage our team to value "the ministry of presence." When people are going through dark times, we never want them to journey alone. Our culture is to come alongside them and just be with them. Words aren't as meaningful as just being there. And in fact, words can get in the way. Is there a time to teach them that God is sovereign and will

28 Danita Bye, *Millennials Matter: Proven Strategies for Building Your Next-Gen Leader* (United States: BroadStreet Publishing Group LLC., 2017), 151.

use even the worst tragedies somehow for good? Yes, but not now. And not soon. And not for a long while. Not until the right moment opens up.

I've noticed that when people get divorced, people who have been friends of the couple either take sides or back away from both of them. The awkwardness can isolate the two getting a divorce even more than the death of a spouse. In those times, they need true friends who are there for them and with them, not enflaming their anger at the offender (and both sides almost always believe they are the victims), but walking with them step by step in their grieving, forgiving, and healing. Hurrying people does more damage. Let people walk at their own pace, wrestling with disappointment with God, their ex, themselves, and former friends who are keeping their distance.

Ministry is messy. Leading people is often compared with herding cats. I get it, but that's our role as leaders. It would be much easier for me to invest all of my time in preparing my messages, preaching, and going into a cocoon where I didn't have to interact with people. But that's not God's calling—for me, for my team, or for any person who serves in our church. After a worship service not long ago, I had finished praying with people at the front and was heading toward the entrance of our sanctuary, and I greeted a few people. An eleven-year-old boy walked up. His Dad stood a few feet behind him. I could tell the boy had something on his mind. I shook his hand and he told me, "Thank you for being our pastor. Thank you for taking time to talk to us . . . to people like me." I smiled and nodded, but he wasn't finished. He then smiled and told me, "Pastor, I want you to know that I filled out one of the cards today. I signed up for reoccurring giving."

I laughed and replied, "Well, let me tell you a story. When I was about your age, my Dad taught me the principles of giving to the Lord. Your commitment today will carry you a long way in the rest of your life." It was a precious moment. I'm so glad this boy had the courage to interact with me.

RUNNING PARTNERS

Success in life is greatly impacted by who you hang out with, or more accurately, who you run with. This is particularly true in tuna fishing. As I have shared with you, tuna are a school fish, so when you are in a school, the fishing is incredible. But you can spend days searching the ocean to find the fish. In tuna fishing, success depends on having partners who can travel with you and spread out to scout a different territory. Running partners contact each other with radios that scramble the messages so they can only decode each other, making it a private channel. These partners go to sea together. They are people who understand the risks you face and the impact of time away from family. Your running partners are also your only protection against threats that may arise at sea. No one else is close enough to make a difference in a time of need. They're also a sounding board for each other. We sometimes talk with each other about how to make a repair of a critical piece of equipment while in the middle of the ocean. On the ocean, running partners are the only people who are committed to your success, your safety, and your ability to return safely to your family.

I have explained the importance of the sacred trust of leadership, shared leadership, but another important aspect of life and ministry is to have people in your life that you run with and together chase the dreams and purposes of God. Remember, all quality ministry flows from relationship.

Today, we face enormous challenges in our culture, including race issues, division, and strife. To see real change, our relationships must go deeper. Our commitment to each other's lives and families has to go deeper. We have to watch out for each other and stay close enough to care and help in times of need.

Many times, we talk about a relationship that can change your life. For me one of the greatest blessings that Jammin' brought was a relationship I developed with Pastor John Jenkins Sr. of First Baptist Church of Glenarden, Maryland. When our NBA friends, along with a pastor in Washington, D.C., invited us to hold an event in the city, it was recommended that we ask John about being the chairperson of the event. I met John and shared the vision of Jammin'. He agreed, and this began one of the most meaningful ministry experiences I've had. We held two years of back-to-back Jammin' events in the nation's capital. The first DC Jammin event had a basketball tournament on Indepence Avenue and a sold out main event in the Verizon Center. The next year we followed up with a basketball tournament on Pennsylvania Avenue and a sold out U.S Air Arena main event. Each year thousands attended and hundreds received Christ. A lot of incredible blessings came out of those two years, but on a personal level, one of the most fulfilling benefits was the amazing bond of friendship between John and me. It's a bond that a lot of people would never expect to happen. Our differences are easy to see: Seattle is predominately white; Washington is predominately Black; we come from very different denominations.

Through the process of working together and facing a lot of challenges, we have come to love and appreciate one another. Far too often, leaders who go to Washington are looking for a photo op, not to minister to the local people. We dealt with all these issues, but we chose the road of respect, taking time to be together, and not just on the business side—we prayed together and had meals together; I stayed in John's home, and we invested in each other's children. We watched each other's kids' sporting events, even though we lived on opposite sides of the country. We each flew across the country and attended our sons' weddings, making time out of demanding schedules to be there for one another. Through it all, John and I discovered that we have more in common than the ways we're different. We became running partners; we had a private channel as we talked about the big things in life.

There is much work to be done to heal the divide in our nation, but the bond of love is the bridge that can bring the change we need.

Later, when we were both going through building programs, we brought the bond of our friendship to our churches, and our friendship demonstrated for our people what could really happen when we set issues aside and choose to live as true brothers. Because of this bond, we've been leaders in our spheres of influence at a deeper level, helping others see, not just the *work* that needs to be done, but *the path of the work* that needs to happen. Just like running partners, we've been a place of safety for each other. Not just a private channel, but we have chosen not to be offended regardless what's happening in our culture—we're not willing for anything to divide us. Our churches are different because of this relationship. The level of respect that our church gives to John when he comes to Eastridge is second to none, and we in turn are showered in love by the First Baptist family. Our kids, because of what they have seen and experienced, have a different expectation and a different experience because of our friendship.

There is much work to be done to heal the divide in our nation, but the bond of love is the bridge that can bring the change we need. I've seen it on my Dad's boat, I've seen it at our church, I've seen it in every Jammin' event, and I've seen it in well-led organizations across the country and around the world: there's nothing so exhilarating and fulfilling as a team pulling together to accomplish something great . . . especially accomplishing something for the glory of God.

> *"People fail to get along because they fear each other; they fear each other because they don't know each other; they don't know each other because they have not communicated with each other."*[29]
> —Martin Luther King Jr.

---

29 L.D. Reddick, *Crusader Without Violence: A Biography of Martin Luther King, Jr.* (Greece: NewSouth Books, 2018)

WHAT'S YOUR PLACE?

I wasn't sure if I should laugh or cry when I heard a man tell me, "Church work looks too easy. It's not enough of a challenge. I don't think it's worth getting involved."

I had one thought for him: you need to get close enough to see what really happens day to day. But thankfully, I said, "Tell me about that. What causes you to think that way?"

He explained that the worship service runs very smoothly and other parts of the organization operate seemingly without a hitch. Since he didn't serve in the church, he hadn't had the opportunity to look behind the curtain to see what's really going on. An enormous amount of work is invested in every ministry of the church. That's why we need teams of people who are devoted first to God and then to each other and God's cause. Together, we trust in the leading of God and the power of the Spirit to accomplish what He has put in front of us. People who look behind the curtain first see the teamwork, shared leadership, creativity, heartfelt prayer, joys, heartaches, and the sacred bond among us. Many people don't see our involvement in the lives of abuse victims, alcoholics and addicts, couples on the verge of divorce, those who have heard a diagnosis that makes them tremble, wayward children, financial strains, and a thousand other problems—messy problems—when we step into their lives to offer comfort and support.

We've all heard the metaphor that a church is like a football game, with thousands of people sitting in the stands to be entertained and a few exhausted players on the field. That's a joke that has more than a taste of reality in it. But it doesn't have to be that way. As a leader, it's my responsibility to create a culture where everybody finds a place to serve ... everybody gets a place on the crew, even if it's for the first trip and they have a lot to learn.

Together, we trust in the leading of God and the power of the Spirit to accomplish what He has put in front of us.

Let me articulate a few concepts to create that kind of culture.

ASK QUESTIONS

Find out what makes your church tick. Who are the leaders and how do they lead? What's the vision? What are the guiding principles? How do volunteers feel about their roles? God has given us the Great Commandment to love Him and love people, and He has given us the Great Commission to share the message of His love to everyone on the planet, making multiplying disciples of those who believe. That doesn't sound "too easy" to me!

LOOK FOR A ROLE THAT'S BOTH FULFILLING AND CHALLENGING

It may take some time, but most of us will eventually find a "Goldilocks role"—not too easy, not too hard, just right. If it's too easy, you'll quickly become bored. If it's too hard, or you don't feel supported, you'll look for something else ... or abandon ship! Don't let that happen. Communicate well and often with the person leading your team. Sometimes a small shift in responsibilities, or perhaps finding additional resources, will make a role much more fulfilling.

The need may be your calling, but not always. Many people are sensitive and compassionate, and they're flexible to use their skills wherever the church leaders need them. But some of us simply don't fit a role we're asked to fill.

BE REALISTIC

Finding the right fit as a volunteer may not happen instantly. Give one role a try. If it fits, stick with it and grow in your skills and capacity. If it doesn't, try something else ... but don't get discouraged in the process. Most of us have tried a number of roles before we found something that rang true in our hearts.

LEARN FROM SUCCESSES AND SETBACKS

Some people assume their service should be expedited, placing them immediately into a leadership position. It's more like being an apprentice, putting yourself under a seasoned leader who will train you and encourage you. On my Dad's boat, the people who had unrealistic assumptions didn't last long, but the ones who were willing to try anything and give it their best always became good fishermen ... and they earned the respect of everyone on the crew.

TAKE THE STEP

If you sense God prompting you, make the move. Get involved. Talk to your leaders and find out the pathway to get involved. You'll have the opportunity to serve and make a difference, and you'll also grow in your relationships with God and His people.

My best advice, dive in; it's much easier to steer a boat when it is moving instead of tied to the dock.

RELATIONSHIPS ARE EVERYTHING

Yes, the fit of skills and interests are important, but the bond created on a team that's working well is pure gold. I don't think that's true only for extroverts; it's true for all of us. Invest in people, on your team, in your church, and in the community. Let love motivate everything you do.

TRUST IS BUILT OVER TIME

We earn our place on the crew as people see our willingness to consistently pitch in. We may not have the consummate skills others possess, but we're FAT: faithful, available, and teachable.

> *"The church is not a theological classroom. It is a conversion, confession, repentance, reconciliation, forgiveness and sanctification center, where flawed people place their faith in Christ, gather to know and love him better, and learn to love others as he designed."*[30]
> —Paul David Tripp

---

30 Paul Tripp, *Dangerous Calling: Confronting the Unique Challenges of Pastoral Ministry.* (United States: Crossway, 2012)

CHAPTER 6
SHARKS, ROCKS, AND DRIFT

"We are locked in a battle. This is not a friendly, gentleman's discussion. It is a life and death conflict between the spiritual hosts of wickedness and those who claim the name of Christ."[31]
—FRANCIS A. SCHAEFFER

In addition to the danger we experienced on my Dad's boat in Pacific storms (which I'll describe in the next chapter), three other threats were constant companions: sharks, underwater rocks, and drifting off course for many miles.

Each year when halibut season ended, we left the frigid waters of Alaska for the warm waters to fish for albacore tuna. I loved fishing tuna, with the warmer weather, and the clear blue waters of the Japanese Current where the tuna migrate. Tuna fishing was the polar opposite of halibut fishing—no more miles of gear, baiting thousands of hooks, or even dressing and icing fish. Now we trolled for tuna, using eleven lines of varying lengths from two huge poles that were part of the boat's mast and rigging.

31 Francis Schaeffer, *The Complete Works of Francis A. Schaeffer: A Christian View of the Church* (United States: Crossway Books, 1982), 316.

The Most Valuable Catch

This species of tuna are smaller than the huge bluefin you see on *Wicked Tuna*. I love albacore; they're a beautiful metallic color with a deep blue top side that blends with the ocean color. They're fast and powerful, swimming up to fifty miles an hour, so when they hit, the action is exhilarating!

Once on deck, our process was simple: we would flash-freeze them by placing them whole into a brine tank on the deck that had the capacity to freeze a ton of fish at a time. The next step would be to drop them into the fish hold below decks and stack them in divided sections of the boat for proper safety.

Another perk of tuna fishing was that we fished during daylight. At night we would shut our main engine down and drift in the seas hundreds of miles from land. The ocean swells would lift and rock the boat, and water would rush across the decks and out the scuppers back into the ocean, carrying blood and fish oil from the tuna still on deck waiting to be frozen.

People always ask about the rough days at sea, but fortunately, there are also many beautiful days on water. I loved nights when the weather was good, because the water is deep blue and crystal clear. (If you've been to Hawaii, you know what I mean.) We had high-powered halogen lights in the rigging that lit up the entire deck and the surrounding water. Sharks can smell blood in the water from a quarter of a mile away at one part per ten billion. In other words, it didn't take much to attract a lot of these predators. Most of the sharks that approached our boat were sleek blue sharks, but at times great whites would also cruise up to let their presence be known. It was always exciting to look at the water and see the halogen lights catch the eyes of the sharks. You could see their eyes twinkle. I have to admit that my fascination with sharks led to a game I played night after night: I tied a small tuna by the tail using a tuna line called a ganoin. I threw the fish as far as I could. As soon as it hit the water, every shark in the vicinity turned and sped to the splash. I pulled the line as fast as I could. The tuna looked like it was water skiing! As the tuna got close to the boat, I yanked it hard and it flew over the side and onto the deck. Some of the sharks jumped with their mouths wide open trying to chomp the tuna in mid-air. It was pretty exciting entertainment for a young man on a fishing boat!

Sharks are a good metaphor for the kind of difficulties that surface when we trust God for great things. It's more than a conceptual challenge to figure out and move on. It's personal. It's an attack by the enemy of our souls. Sharks are naturally attracted to blood in the water or struggling fish. In the same way, Satan is naturally attracted to believers who are giving everything they've got to honor God. Sometimes leaders can get knocked off course because of an attack of the enemy or just obstacles that hinders their work. I want you to know this doesn't mean you're missing it or out of the will of God. In fact, every great work of God won't just be opposed, it will be attacked. In one of His more well-known statements, Jesus contrasted His heart for us with Satan's. He loves, protects, guides, and provides . . . but our enemy? He has a very different goal. Jesus explained the difference, "Very truly I tell you, I am the gate for the sheep. All who have come before me are thieves and robbers, but the sheep have not listened to them. I am the gate; whoever enters through me will be saved. They will come in and go out, and find pasture. The thief comes only to steal and kill and destroy; I have come that they may have life, and have it to the full" (John 10:7-10).

Opposition is just as much a part of a movement of God as blessings. Expect it, and you won't be caught off guard.

"There is no neutral ground in the universe; every square inch, every split second is claimed by God and counterclaimed by Satan."[32]
—C. S. Lewis

As you are seeking God to hear His voice in your life, especially when you are facing attacks, it is important to know that you can trust the Holy Spirit to lead and guide you. Don't operate in fear, but go to the source of your strength and allow Him to lead you.

At one point in the history of our church, we had been in a long process of developing a new ministry campus in Issaquah. (I'll share more about this in a later chapter.) We had spent about five million dollars on site development and our foundation. When we were ready to raise the walls, we discovered a structural engineering error—the weight-bearing beams were all undervalued. In other words, the building would have been in danger of collapse from day one! The project had to be redesigned and peer reviewed, and then we had to go back to the county for reapproval. In this extended process, the economy in 2008-2009 began to crater. Our financing was through a top church lender. To my surprise, the lender's CEO called to tell us that they were closing down all projects across the country, including ours. This was devastating news. How could we survive sitting on a five-million-dollar hole in the ground? Our people had been faithful for years to see this ministry expansion, and now it was all at risk. The CEO pointed

32 C.S. Lewis, *Christian Reflection* (United States: Wm. B. Eerdmans Publishing, 2014), 33.

to the economy, and he also explained that we would need to have the project rebid because of the engineering problem. I told him I felt our team was close to having a new contract ready. He didn't seem to believe that could be true. He gave me three days to send him a new contract.

When I got off the phone, I called our business director and asked for a progress report. I asked, "Can we get it all buttoned down in two days?"

He answered, "We're close. We'll give it all we have!" I called the CEO's office the next day and asked for an appointment. He agreed, so I and several others flew fly to Los Angeles to meet with him.

We entered the bank's conference room and saw an eleven-point agenda in front of each seat. Every point addressed issues related to the closing down of our project. To the surprise of the CEO, our team presented a signed contract and fulfillment of other demands he'd made. The executive and his team were shocked with the quality of our new contractor and the new contract.

He left the room to talk to his team. When he came back, he said, "We've been in such a difficult place shutting down church projects. A lot of pastors and their teams haven't followed up to do what they said they would do, but you guys have. We just need one more thing for your project to go forward. We need to know that your people are still committed to this project in the midst of this recession. To show good faith, we need you to give us an additional one million dollars in four weeks."

I told him, "Okay, we'll go to work on it."

I went home to meet with our board and our congregation on Sunday to share the news. The next few weeks, our building fund offerings were at their lowest point, around five thousand dollars a week. One day, I could tell that this pressure was having an effect on Cheryl. I asked her, "What's giving you the most stress?"

She replied, "I think you're going to lose your job."

I told her, "I'm not worried about losing my job. After all, who would want this job right now?"

Then she asked another striking question, one I was also asking myself: "How do you go from five thousand dollars to a million dollars?"

My response was simple: "Our people are praying. We've honored God as a church in a sacrificial way, sowing into church plants and missions. Our reliance has always been on God's faithfulness alone."

But Cheryl was right. From a human point of view, things didn't look good at all. We held a miracle offering on the Sunday just before the deadline. When that day came, our church's future was on the line. We were stunned as people came in and gave with a spirit of vision and joy. After the service, no one left because they waited to hear the results, and to our amazement and delight, the offering was $1.27 million in cash, a used Honda, and a piece of land. It was an unforgettable day of faith and generosity as our people were investing in what matters most, reaching this generation for Christ.

Check out the spontaneous joy and celebration at First Baptist Church of Glenarden, to hearing of Eastridge's million dollar offering.

"If [Jesus] is who he says he is, he must become the still point of your turning world, the center around which your entire life revolves."[33]
—Tim Keller

A second threat is submerged rocks. The coastline of Alaska doesn't look like the smooth beaches of Florida. In many places, the mountains come right down to the water. Rocky islands are found the entire length of the shore, and the rocks don't stop at the shoreline. Years of navigating these waters have given captains information about the dangers of barely submerged obstacles. Channels are clearly marked, but some skippers assume the placid water on top means there's nothing underneath. Or in many cases, they believe they can beat the odds and take a shortcut and make it through. It can be a very costly mistake.

Off the north coast of Washington, the stretch of water between the mainland tip called Cape Flattery and Tatoosh Island looks navigable, but the buoys and charts take boats hours out of the way to avoid underwater obstacles. It seems like a waste of time . . . until you do an online search of the shipwrecks of Tatoosh Island—there's a reason for a famous lighthouse on the island!

There are plenty of submerged rocks in our lives. We see it all around us: people who have reached tremendous heights in business, sports, entertainment, and ministry who feel as if the rules don't apply to them. They're sure they can beat the odds, only to discover that the rocks just under the water are bigger than they are. We have all witnessed incredibly gifted people in business and ministry bring destruction upon themselves. They

---

33 Tim Keller, *Jesus the King: Understanding the Life and Death of the Son of God* (United States, Penguin Books, 2016), 48.

wreck what they've worked to build, and in many cases, they've lost the most valuable treasure—their families.

In every area and every vocation, the rules are there to prevent us from catastrophic wrecks. We may notice the rocks sometimes, but at high tide, they're hidden beneath the surface. Every temptation looks attractive on the surface, but we pay a high price for ignoring the warning signs. The Bible is full of "channel markers" to show us the way and warn us of danger. For instance, in Matthew 23, Jesus issues a series of warnings to the Pharisees about their hard hearts and hypocrisy. And in John's first letter, he reminds his readers of several hidden dangers: "Do not love the world or anything in the world. If anyone loves the world, love for the Father is not in them. For everything in the world—the lust of the flesh, the lust of the eyes, and the pride of life—comes not from the Father but from the world. The world and its desires pass away, but whoever does the will of God lives forever" (1 John 2:15–17). The biblical concept of idolatry isn't just about stone or wood carvings; it's anything that takes God's rightful place in our hearts, such as power, approval, wealth, control, pleasure, or sexual allure. Those things (and countless other pursuits) aren't necessarily wrong if they're secondary, but when we make them our supreme value, we inevitably crash.

A third threat is drift. In our "second season," my Dad was meticulous in the preparation to find tuna. Actually, it's called "tuna chasing" because we might catch them in one spot one day but they're gone the next. On one particular trip, we were catching a lot of tuna when a fierce storm blew in. It was too dangerous for us to be on deck or fish, so we had to tie everything down, "batten down the hatches," and put up our gear until the storm quieted down. We drifted at the mercy of the wind and waves, and the next morning we were sixty miles from where we started. Dad found our position on the chart and guided us back. It took us a full day of pounding into the waves to get back where the tuna were biting, but the effort was necessary for us to catch fish.

It's easy for us to drift off course and find ourselves a long way from where we really want to be. We can try alcohol or experiment with drugs, we can be controlled by food (or the lack of food), gambling, shopping, and any of a hundred other things. Some of these take a long time for us to turn around and come back to the place where we started drifting, but no matter how far we're off course, now is the time to start the journey back. We can suffer another type of drift when, over an extended period of time, we're exhausted, bored, or unappreciated. Our vision becomes cloudy, and our passion evaporates. The Bible calls this "losing heart," and it's a danger for all of us, even (maybe especially) those who have been deeply involved in serving Christ for many years. Paul's remedy was to focus our attention on the end result of our obedience and realize that perseverance is worth it. He wrote the believers in Corinth:

"Therefore we do not lose heart. Though outwardly we are wasting away, yet inwardly we are being renewed day by day. For our light and momentary troubles are achieving for us an eternal glory that far outweighs them all. So we fix our eyes not on what is seen, but on what is unseen, since what is seen is temporary, but what is unseen is eternal"—2 Corinthians 4:16–18

Sharks, rocks, and drift. They may be connected to storms, but they can also happen on a sunny day. If we're not alert and prepared, any of them can prevent us from fulfilling the vision God has given us . . . at least until we grow wiser and better prepared.

OUT OF THE ASHES

When Katie Mathews was sixteen, she was riding with a friend on the highway. Her friend was distracted and nearly missed the exit but swerved to try to make the turn. The car skidded sideways and rolled over four times. Katie was severely injured, on the brink of death. A couple of paramedics were traveling in the opposite direction and saw the crash. They quickly turned around and got to Katie in time to save her life, but at the hospital, the doctors told her she wouldn't recover movement in her arms and legs. This perfectly healthy teenager had, in an instant, become a quadriplegic. She was as crushed in spirit as she was in body, and she spiraled into the depths of resentment and self-pity.

Her mother refused to give up on her future, so one day she told Katie, "You can stay devastated, or you can see the possibilities for a better future and start moving toward it." This was the wakeup call Katie needed. Through her suffering, she believed in Jesus and trusted Him to make something beautiful of her broken life. Now, years later, she is one of the sweetest, most optimistic people I know, a breath of fresh air to everyone around her. Katie speaks in high schools about the dangers of distracted driving. Her wheelchair gives her instant credibility.

Katie's is a tremendous example for us of the importance of seeking God in our places of pain and uncertainty. She has developed a heart in pursuit of God and the result is she has found meaning and purpose in her life. She has joined the team at Providence Heights, an organization dedicated to help women so they don't fall into homelessness, sparing them the pain and shame that usually accompanies that condition.

THAT'LL LEAVE A MARK

After John Mark left them, Paul and Barnabas continued their trip into the heart of today's Turkey. Paul's message in the synagogue in Pisidian Antioch is a classic. For his Jewish listeners (and for us) he connected the gospel of Jesus to their treasured history of Abraham, David, and God's purposes for the nation of Israel. When they left the city, they continued to Iconium, where again Paul preached in the synagogue. A lot of Jewish people trusted in Jesus, "But the Jews who refused to believe stirred up the other Gentiles and poisoned their minds against the brothers" (Acts 14:2). Paul and Barnabas kept speaking out, and God confirmed their message with signs and wonders. The opposition wasn't going to take this, so they conspired to capture them and stone them to death. The two men fled and went down the road to Lystra. They hoped for a better reception there.

The scene Luke describes in Lystra is one of the most dramatic—and strange—in his history of the early church. When the two men entered the city, they noticed a man who was lame, and in fact, had been lame all his life. Paul sensed the man had faith to be healed, so he commanded him, "Stand up on your feet!" (Acts 14:10) The man jumped up and began to walk!

This miracle hadn't taken place in secret. A crowd of people had observed it, and they concluded, "The gods have come down to us in human form!" (v. 11) They believed Barnabas was the Greek god Zeus and Paul was Hermes, the spokesman. Then, something even more amazing happened: "The priest of Zeus, whose temple was just outside the city, brought bulls and wreaths to the city gates because he and the crowd wanted to offer sacrifices to them" (Acts 14:13).

We all want others to appreciate us, don't we? But this was way over the top! Luke takes us to the moment:

But when the apostles Barnabas and Paul heard of this, they tore their clothes and rushed out into the crowd, shouting: "Friends, why are you doing this? We too are only human, like you. We are bringing you good news, telling you to turn from these worthless things to the living God, who made the heavens and the earth and the sea and everything in them. In the past, he let all nations go their own way. Yet he has not left himself without testimony: He has shown kindness by giving you rain from heaven and crops in their seasons; he provides you with plenty of food and fills your hearts with joy." Even with these words, they had difficulty keeping the crowd from sacrificing to them. —Acts 14:14–18

Crisis averted. They obviously had people's attention, and now they could spend time teaching them more about Jesus ... except that's not what happened. At that moment, some of the hostile Jews from Antioch and Iconium showed up. They told the crowd that Paul and Barnabas were imposters, and the crowd that was ready to sacrifice bulls to them stoned Paul and dragged him out of the city! (Luke doesn't tell us where Barnabas was, but since Paul was the chief presenter, the crowd's wrath was centered on him.)

Paul was lifeless on the ground. Stoning is a particularly brutal means of execution. Large stones are hurled at the person's head and body, breaking bones and cracking the skull. The people who had believed Paul's message stood over him, and I'm sure they prayed. They may have committed his soul to God and prepared to bury him, but Paul got up! And then, maybe the strangest thing of all happened: He went back into the city to tell more people about Jesus! (I can imagine Barnabas and the new believers shaking their heads and thinking, *Wow, what a gutsy move!*)

Paul and Barnabas endured personal hostility. They had no idea performing a miracle would cause such a violent reaction (sharks and rocks), but they didn't drift away from God's clear calling.

PAY ATTENTION

The Holy Spirit is active in preparing us to face all three threats. If we're serious about making a difference for God, the enemy will attack us—that's his nature. If we think we can cut corners, wink at sin, and get away with giving in to temptation ("just this once"), we'll hit the rocks under the water and cause a lot of damage. And when we drift—and we all do from time to time—we have the choice to keep drifting or do the hard work of regaining the ground we've lost, focusing our attention on the benefits and blessings in the future instead of dreading the hard work it takes today to get back where we need to be.

The Christian life is much more than concepts and morals. The Spirit of God wants to assure us, lead us, and provide for us. We may sometimes feel isolated, but we're never alone. He is as close as our breath and kinder and stronger than we can imagine. One of the Spirit's chief roles in our lives is to convince us that we belong to Him. The doctrine of justification is wonderful—we're "in Christ" in His death, so we're completely forgiven, and we're "in Christ" in His perfect life, so His righteousness is credited to us. Paul explains "the great swap" that Jesus took the judgment for our sins, and He has given us the status of righteousness: "God made [Jesus] who had no sin to be sin for us, so that in him we might become the righteousness of God (2 Corinthians 5:21). Those are the fundamental truths of the gospel, but there's more. The Judge who declared us "not guilty" because Jesus has already paid the price for us has taken off His robe and adopted us into His family. In his letter to the Romans, Paul describes this life-changing relationship and the Spirit's role in assuring us that it's true:

> *For those who are led by the Spirit of God are the children of God. The Spirit you received does not make you slaves, so that you live in fear again; rather, the Spirit you received brought about your adoption to sonship. And by him we cry, "Abba, Father." The Spirit himself testifies with our spirit that we are God's children. Now if we are children, then we are heirs—heirs of God and co-heirs with Christ, if indeed we share in his sufferings in order that we may also share in his glory. —Romans 8:14–17*

God communicates with His children. That's what loving parents do with their kids. I've heard people say, "Well, God doesn't speak to me. There may be something wrong with me or wrong with God, but I don't hear anything." In the spiritual realm, "speaking" happens in different ways. As we saw in the opening chapter, God communicates with us in many ways, but primarily through His Word. When we read it, meditate on it, and let it sink into our hearts, we're "hearing" His voice speak to us. And of course, the Spirit has many other means of communicating, but I've noticed that if someone isn't regularly studying the Bible, they seldom sense God leading them in any other way.

〰〰〰〰〰〰〰〰〰〰〰〰〰〰〰〰〰〰〰〰

If we're serious about making a difference for God, the enemy will attack us—that's his nature.

It's tempting to take shortcuts in our relationship with God. It's like a captain who relies exclusively on GPS to navigate. That's fine, but it's important to also chart the course on a map. When the GPS system goes down or the connection is spotty, the captain will still know where he is and the heading to the next destination.

The news is peppered with stories of men and women who weren't ready for opposition, who took shortcuts and hit the rocks, and who drifted into temptations they never dreamed would be a problem for them. In ministry, business, higher education, and every other field, the landscape is cluttered with people who didn't pay attention.

"Talent is a gift but character is a choice. We don't get to pick our talents or IQ but we do choose our character. In fact, we create it every time we make choices to cop out or dig out of a hard situation, to bend the truth or stand under the weight of it."[34]
—John C. Maxwell

A commitment to integrity protects us from all kinds of heartaches. George Reese worked as a carpenter for a construction

---

34 John Maxwell, *The 21 Indispensable Qualities of a Leader: Becoming the Person Others Will Want to Follow* (United States: T. Nelson, 2007), 4.

company. He was very good at his work, and the company promoted him to run one of their divisions.

Every few weeks one of the two company owners (partners) would travel to see George and the operation. One day, he got a call from the partners saying they were both going to make a trip to see him. This caused George some concern, simply because it had never happened before. They picked him up and drove to a local restaurant. When they walked in, the partners asked for a booth that had no one sitting near it. They started their conversation by telling George that they were impressed with his work and his attitude. They asked him a number of questions, and then their next statement caught George off guard: they told George the company was facing a "legal difficulty." They explained that they may need him to do the company a favor and "tell a little story to help the company. Can we count on you, George?"

George sensed that this question wasn't about normal business practices of being careful not to waste resources. It appeared that they were asking him to compromise his ethical integrity. He asked a few questions to be sure he understood what they were asking. When it was clear, he sensed the Holy Spirit whisper, "This isn't who you are. This isn't what you're committed to be and do."

The offer of a lifetime was on the table, but George told them, "No, I won't do that. I won't do anything to compromise my integrity."

One of them smiled and said, "Your response is exactly what we were looking for. Our company is based on integrity, and we wanted to see if you're as committed to integrity as we are. It has taken years to build our reputation. People trust us, and we won't do anything to jeopardize that trust. George, you passed the test. Welcome to ownership. We're glad you're a partner on our team."

George left for work that morning as an employee and came home an owner. His financial future was transformed by keeping his heart on what matters most. Eventually, George became the CEO of the company, and it has thrived under his leadership. When Cheryl and I moved to the area and needed to find a home, we talked to George. We live in a house his company built.

Your temptation and mine may not be exactly like the one George faced when the owners of the company tested him, but we face them again and again. In each one, we have to choose, sometimes in an instant, if we'll listen to the voice of God and live with integrity . . . or give in to the enemy's schemes, take shortcuts, or drift away from God's best.

Sometimes, we need God's discernment to figure out the nature of a threat. A few years ago, a couple started attending our church. As I got to know them, he told me that he owned a hedge fund that was making a lot of money. The wife had a tender heart, and they both expressed their excitement about being part of a church that was doing so much to reach the lost and help people grow in their faith. They took other members of our staff and me to lunch, and they expressed their desire to get to know us better. The couple invited Cheryl and me to their home, and he took me into his garage to show me his Lamborghini. It was a beautiful car, but his need to impress me gave me concern. His greatest desire, he explained, was to use his money to build the kingdom of God. He told me, "I hope that in the near future, I'll walk into your office and present you with a check for $10 million for the church." If the motives were pure, what pastor wouldn't love to hear that?

One day as we met for lunch, he said, "Steve, my company has a lot of resources to help people in the church. If you'll give me the names and contact information of the top donors, I'll show them how they can maximize their giving to advance God's kingdom at our church."

Instantly, I sensed a red light flashing in my heart: Watch out! It was the Holy Spirit warning me that this guy wasn't who he claimed to be. The previous months of interaction had been an elaborate scam to get me to trust him, and all of his pronouncements of wanting to advance God's kingdom were his attempts to get me to lower my guard. So, I told him right then that I would not be able to share any information on our members or donors. After we met, I went to the office of our business manager, who had been developing quite a friendship with the guy. I told him about the conversation and said, "I want to give him every opportunity to prove me wrong, but I believe he's a fraud. If he'll keep coming to church and participate in our discipleship program and serve with us over the long haul, I'm glad for him to be with us. But there are no shortcuts, and we don't make special arrangements for people who have money … or who claim to have money." This is where our sacred trust of leadership is unmovable.

Trust can't be created without proximity, and discernment won't be accepted without a significant measure of trust.

I didn't want to share my perspective too broadly, but I confided in our board members and our staff team. I wanted them to avoid falling for the smooth talk and grand promises.

A few weeks later, the story hit all of our local media that that the guy and his wife had been arrested by the FBI for fraud. I wish that had been the end of it, but it wasn't. As the investigation brought things to light, I discovered that a number of prominent business executives had invested millions in this guy's hedge fund, and some pastors were listed as victims of the fraud. The offer had sounded really good, but they hadn't realized it was literally too good to be true.

As I look back on our experience with the couple, I'm grateful for many things. We had spent years developing deep layers of trust among our staff and board, so when I warned our leadership team about my concerns, they trusted me enough to take it seriously. I'm thankful that this encounter didn't cause ruptures in our relationships, and in fact, the experience strengthened our bonds even more. Together, we'd faced the threat of a submerged rock, and we steered away from any harm.

Trust can't be created without proximity, and discernment won't be accepted without a significant measure of trust. This is how the body of Christ is meant to function, but today many miss out on what could happen in their spiritual lives because they don't get the benefit of "iron sharpening iron" relationships, especially if the pieces of iron seldom connect. Coming to worship is important so we can feel that we're part of something much bigger than ourselves, hear God's Word, and experience the presence of God together. It's also important to be involved in a close community of people who are encouraging and challenging each other to grow spiritually. We can participate in a small Bible study or serve on a team. That's where we get to know each other, take steps to be vulnerable and open, pray specifically for needs, and do something together that has a tangible impact on others. We can help each other navigate the sometimes rough waters of marriage and raising kids, or figure out how to relate to aging parents. We can provide encouragement about managing finances, and we can support each other when we suffer health problems. And through it all, we discover the beauty of loving one another, being there when the chips are down, and celebrating the joys of walking with God.

> *"Character, morality and ethics are the*
> *foundational principles of leadership."* [35]
> —Dave Ulrich, Norm Smallwood,
> and Kate Sweetman

GET READY, STAY READY

Sharks, rocks, and drift are common phenomenon for fishing boats, and they're common for believers, too.

C. S. Lewis once commented that we often make one of two mistakes in our grasp of spiritual conflict: we either give Satan too much credit, or we give him too little. In America, the vast majority of believers are in the latter category. We need to be informed and prepared for the inevitable attacks of the enemy. Earlier, we looked at Peter's admonition to leaders to shepherd their people with good and godly motives. Immediately after this passage, he warns his readers, "Be alert and of sober mind. Your enemy the devil prowls around like a roaring lion looking

---

35 Dave Ulrich, Norm Smallwood, and Kate Sweetman, *The Leadership Code: Five Rules to Lead By* (United States: Harvard Business Review Press, 2009), 146.

for someone to devour. Resist him, standing firm in the faith, because you know that the family of believers throughout the world is undergoing the same kind of sufferings" (1 Peter 5:8-9).

The devil has three primary strategies: temptation, deception, and accusation. In temptation, he makes sin look more attractive than the blessings of obeying God. In deception, he insists that right is wrong and wrong is right, confusing us about God's nature and purposes. And in accusation, he uses our inner voice to call us horrible names and shame us. If our attention is on what despicable people we are, we won't experience the grace, goodness, and greatness of God.

To combat the enemy's strategies, God has given us the power of truth. Paul explained this fact to the Christians in Corinth:

"For though we live in the world, we do not wage war as the world does. The weapons we fight with are not the weapons of the world. On the contrary, they have divine power to demolish strongholds. We demolish arguments and every pretension that sets itself up against the knowledge of God, and we take captive every thought to make it obedient to Christ"
—2 Corinthians 10:3–5

Make no mistake: we're in a fight. Paul uses the language of warfare—fight, weapons, power, strongholds, demolish, and captive—to illustrate the kind of siege warfare common in the Roman world. This means we examine the thoughts in our heads, evaluate their source, and replace the ones that don't tap into God's truth. Let me offer a few suggestions to help you be prepared.

BE AWARE OF YOUR PATTERNS OF TEMPTATIONS

We're not all the same. Each of us is more tempted to one sin than another. Do your daydreams drift to winning the lottery, paying back someone who hurt you, enjoying riches and pleasure, or delighting in sexual exploits? These are just a few of countless temptations. If you can identify your usual pattern, you'll be more alert so you don't succumb to Satan's strategies, hidden dangers, or gradual drift away from God's heart.

THE ROCKS OF RESENTMENT CAN SINK YOUR BOAT

There's nothing wrong with being angry at injustice, including any injustice directed toward you, but if we don't handle it well, anger quickly festers into resentment and bitterness. Then, our minds dwell on the wrong done to us . . . and the payback the offender deserves. Pastor Frederick Buechner commented:

"Of the Seven Deadly Sins, anger is possibly the most fun. To lick your wounds, to smack your lips over grievances long past, to roll over your tongue the prospect of bitter confrontations still to come, to savor to the last toothsome morsel both the pain you are given and the pain you are giving back—in many ways it is a feast fit for a king. The chief drawback is that what you are wolfing down is yourself. The skeleton at the feast is you!"[36]

Many Christians sing praises on Sunday morning but live with an undercurrent of resentment. Their bitterness gives them two things they desperately want: identity and energy. They see themselves as the victim, the one who was wronged, and their bitterness gives them an ongoing shot of adrenaline that keeps the fires hot.

---

36 Frederick Buechner, *Wishful Thinking* (Harper San Francisco, 1993), 2.

~~~~~~

The Holy Spirit longs to illuminate God's Word and prompt us with whispers and nudges.

The Christian faith is based on the foundation of God's gracious forgiveness. If we can't forgive others, it probably means we haven't experienced God's forgiveness deeply enough. What comes out of us is an overflow of what's in our hearts. Pay attention to the overflow.

SHARPEN THE HOOKS

The Holy Spirit longs to illuminate God's Word and prompt us with whispers and nudges. As we've seen, these are the hooks that connect us with God. We sharpen those hooks by obeying when He prompts us, and we dull them when we resist. Of course, none of us responds perfectly all the time. God is amazingly patient with us, but we have the choice to respond in faith or not.

On my Dad's boat, staying alert to dangers wasn't just his responsibility. Every member of the crew needed to be "always on": noticing how the equipment was operating, anticipating any problems, and mentally staying one step ahead of every action. In the same way, we can't assume it's entirely the pastor's job to be on the lookout for problems. Each of us in the body of Christ is responsible to be "always on," deepening our dependence on God, marveling at His grace in personal and corporate worship, making good decisions about how we invest our time and money, and being ruthlessly honest about the presence of sharks, rocks, and drift in our own lives.

> *"When wealth is lost, nothing is lost; when health is lost, something is lost; when character is lost, all is lost."*[37]
> —Billy Graham

---

37 *Newsweek* Magazine, August 24, 1987, 11.

CHAPTER 7

STORMS ON THE SEA

"We never need to shout across the spaces to an absent
God. He is nearer than our own soul."[38]
—A.W. TOZER

It's one thing to endure howling winds and torrential rain when you're safe in your home; it's something quite different to be on a boat in those conditions, coupled with twenty-foot waves and hundreds of miles from the nearest port. I'd been in plenty of storms on trips with my Dad, but none like this one.

When I was eighteen, Dad and I were fishing for tuna off the coast of Oregon. We knew we were getting into heavy seas, so heavy that we couldn't fish. To get some sleep, I went down to the berth and packed life jackets around me to keep from falling out of the bunk. Early the next morning, I heard Dad yell, "Steve, I need you!" This wasn't a casual, "Hey, son, when you get a minute, I could use a little help. We have fish on the line." This was urgent!

38 A. W. Tozer, *The Pursuit of God: The Human Thirst for the Divine* (United States: Moody Publishers, 2015), 51.

I jumped out of my bunk and rushed onto the deck. I was wearing only my boxers. The boat was struggling in the wind and waves, and Dad was in full rain gear, waist-deep in the water. A huge swell had crashed over the sides. I could see that all the ropes holding down the main hatch had snapped when a wave hit it. The eight-by-eight-foot, heavy wooden top was sitting ajar over the hold. We were about to lose the hatch to the open ocean! (The hatch was tied down for the entire fishing trip, but it had a smaller hatch in the center where we slid the fish down into the hold. The hatch itself was supposed to be completely secure. It only came off when the trip was over and we were back at port. Then we opened it and hoisted the fish out of the hold.)

I had a flashback of an event that had happened on an earlier trip. In a fierce storm, one of the crew opened the lid of our commercial freezer on the flying bridge. It had a heavy wooden cover on top with large industrial hinges, but when he opened it, the wind caught the lid and ripped it completely off the hinges. I watched it fly into the rough seas below. Now in this moment with the decks filled with water we could be just one wave away from our main hatch being washed overboard. If it was, we could be lost at sea.

I'm sure it would have been an exciting picture for National Geographic or the Discovery Channel, but we weren't thinking about the optics. Dad in his rain gear and me in my boxers—both of us were waist-deep in water with the boat heaving one way and then the other. We had one goal: to keep the hatch from going overboard. And if we could do that, we'd have to get new ropes to tie it back down. It was life or death. Neither of us said a word. It was obvious what we needed to do, and we instinctively worked together to make it happen.

He [God] was teaching me the importance of not giving up because things seem impossible or because they're painful.

Today, people sometimes ask me about my spiritual gifts. I tell them that I'm pretty sure my primary gift isn't one that's listed in any of the four New Testament passages. It's perseverance. God must have used the fishing trips with my Dad to instill this trait in me. It may surprise people, but I got seasick on nearly every fishing trip. But I had to stay on deck and do my job with the rest of the crew, hook for hook, fish for fish. I sometimes went days without eating, simply because I knew the food would make a quick roundtrip. It was a challenge to my core, fighting to keep up twenty hours a day with no food. My crew mates felt bad but there was nothing they could do it; was a lonely harsh battle. I didn't realize it at the time, but God was forging something in me that would shape my leadership for the rest of my life. He was teaching me the importance of not giving up because things seem impossible or because they're painful. It would be a few years later, when leading citywide Jammin' outreaches, that I would face challenges even greater than the pain and misery of Alaska.

Cheryl and I have also learned that in pastoring a church and helping build a greater future, we would need a tenacious faith.

As Christians we are going to face difficult moments when we wonder if we can make it through the pain. Sam Chand gives incredible insight to what really happens in leadership. In his book *Leadership Pain*, he explains:

> "*Change only happens when our level of desire (or actually desperation) rises above the level of our fears. . . . The art of leadership is understanding what you can't compromise on.*" He also says, "*Reluctance to face pain is your greatest limitation. There is no growth without change, no change without loss, and no loss without pain.*"[39]

A SMOLDERING PIT

Everyone remembers where they were when they heard the staggering news on September 11, 2001. The year before, we had held a major Jammin' event in Madison Square Garden, and now, pastors who met each other working on that outreach found each other shoulder to shoulder at Ground Zero. They called and asked if I could come and help draw in more pastors.

I arrived in New York, but on the first night I couldn't get closer than six blocks to Ground Zero because of National Guard roadblocks. The next day I was given an all-access pass. We went into devastation like I've never seen. I-beams were stuck in the sides of buildings and the firetrucks constantly tried to knock down the flames. Firefighters gave us yellow hard hats with "I love NY" stickers on them. We walked and prayed with relief workers. The

---

39 Samuel Chand, *Leadership Pain* (United States: Thomas Nelson, 2015), 234.

rescue phase was over but it would be a long time for the recovery efforts to be completed. As I stood in the smoldering pit with my heart broken, I felt the Holy Spirit speak to me that even in these ashes, God was at work. Grace was being poured out over our nation, and that a year from that day was going to be very important. The city and our nation would have to stop and reflect on the grace of God in the midst of the pain.

I left Ground Zero and caught a cab to go uptown to Madison Square Garden. I called a leader at the Garden who had become a friend through our previous event. As I arrived, I told him I wanted to rent the Garden on 9-11 next year. I asked, "Is it available?" The answer was "yes," so I signed a contract along with the MSG executives and gave a deposit.

In the next few weeks, God began to draw together a great coalition of leaders to see this event come to pass, including Pastor A.R. Bernard, Pastor Tom Mahairas, Pastors Rick and Jeremy Del Rio, Pastor Marc Rivera, and Hubie Synn. We agreed to name the event, "A Tribute to Grace and Hope." The plans were coming together to see an event bring hope and healing to the city.

On February 14, I received a call I will never forget. It was someone in leadership at the Garden. He said they believed September 11, 2002, the first anniversary of the attack, was going to be a significant date, too important for a religious event, so they were going to take back the date and help me find a replacement date for our event.

I replied, "I can't agree to that because it's not just about me. In a few weeks, 350 pastors and leaders are coming to a launch event, and Mayor Bloomberg will be there."

He was adamant: "We're not asking. We're telling you!"

They sent me a letter offering a discount on any other date and returned our check. This was a time of incredible pressure on me. What was I to do? I knew God had given me this prompt—it was the same sense of God's direction I had felt as a youth pastor praying through the night. I was on my face, and so was Cheryl. We sought God together.

At times you will feel tremendous pressure. It doesn't mean you're out of the will of God. It just means the final story is still being written.

We had a clear sense that God confirmed His leading to have our event on September 11, not any other date. I respected the Garden and didn't want to break our relationship, so I wrote a nice letter and sent the check back.

A few days later, I received a letter from the Garden rejecting the date again, and they included the check. Once again, questions filled my heart. I felt profound disappointment and sheer stress. I think many times when people would attend a Jammin' event, and the place was rocking with fun, and then the altar call brought hundreds forward, they assumed it was "an easy win." The truth was that behind each outreach, we agonized in prayer with the pressures that came with it.

The check went back and forth three times. Just as I was ready to give up and start looking for another venue, the Lord impressed me: "No, send it back again," and He gave me five points to share. I sent the letter and the check, and a few days later, my phone rang. It was the leaders of Madison Square Garden. They informed me that they didn't concede to any of my points, but they decided the best use was for us to have the arena on September 11.

At times you will feel tremendous pressure. It doesn't mean you're out of the will of God. It just means the final story is still being written.

By standing on conviction in the midst of the storm, breakthroughs began to come. My NBA friends, Allan Houston and Charlie Ward, along with Michael Barrow of the New York Giants, stood by me in the preparation and later spoke at the event to share their faith in Jesus and their love for the city. Musicians Toby Mac, Third Day, Steven Curtis Chapman, Fred Hammond, and Marcos Witt joined the team to provide music. Firefighters and police officers who survived the collapse shared their experiences of how God helped them in the moment. Widows and family members who lost loved ones shared their stories of God being with them in the midst of their grief, and local pastors came together to speak of the grace and hope that Jesus brought in the midst of the storm.

Christian television networks TBN and Daystar stepped in to broadcast the event on satellites circling the globe. On that day, a massive windstorm hit the city. Each borough had scheduled outdoor concerts with some of the biggest names in entertainment, but every concert had to be canceled because of the storm.

Just hours before the Garden opened, Time Warner called and asked if it was true that we were having a live 9/11 event from the Garden. I said, "Yes, we are." They replied, "If you can give us a feed, we'll broadcast it to millions of homes."

That night I preached on the power of the cross (referencing the twisted steel beams pulled out of the rubble by construction workers), and how, when all else is destroyed, God can bring hope out of the ashes. I gave an altar call, inviting people to open their lives to Jesus, and people from all over the arena flooded the altar to the point that there just wasn't room for everyone.

This moment of salvation stretched live around the world and then was rebroadcast numerous times. This incredible time of salvation began a year earlier in a smoldering pit with just a prompt of the Holy Spirit. But a tremendous spiritual battle took place on many levels trying to hinder God's plans. It took a desperate reliance on the Holy Spirit every step of the way.

You may be standing in a storm and wondering if you should just give up. You may be tempted to give up on your marriage, a friend, or even yourself. I know it hurts to breathe sometimes, and you're worn out, but don't give up. Instead, give in and surrender it all to God. He can handle your needs. God's grace and love are greater than the ashes that may be surrounding you right now.

> *"Many of life's failures are people who did not realize*
> *how close they were to success when they gave up."*[40]
> —Thomas Edison

NOT THIS TIME!

One of the more disconcerting stories in Luke's account of the early church is the unresolved argument between Barnabas and

---

40 Deborah Hedstrom-Page, *From Telegraph to Light Bulb with Thomas Edison* (United States: B&H Books, 2007), 22.

Paul. The two had been inseparable, trusted partners in launching Jesus's revolutionary movement, but a storm hit them.

The believers in Antioch had been strengthened by Paul's teaching and Barnabas's encouragement, and with a fresh vision, they commissioned them to take the gospel where it had not been heard. Paul and Barnabas took the young man, John Mark, Barnabas's cousin, with them. They first sailed to Cyprus, where Barnabas was from. They preached in the Jewish synagogues in Salamis and Paphos. In that city, they encountered a Jewish sorcerer and false prophet named Bar-Jesus, who opposed their ministry. Paul, full of the Spirit, told the sorcerer:

"You are a child of the devil and an enemy of everything that is right! You are full of all kinds of deceit and trickery. Will you never stop perverting the right ways of the Lord? Now the hand of the Lord is against you. You are going to be blind for a time, not even able to see the light of the sun."—Acts 13:10-11

Instantly, the man was blinded, which amazed the leader of the city.

Pretty impressive ... but perhaps more than a little scary. When the three arrived at Perga on the southern coast of today's Turkey, John Mark left them and returned to Jerusalem. Luke gives us no more explanation than the bare facts, but we find out more after the missionary trip ends and Paul and Barnabas prepare for their second journey.

God accomplished amazing things on the first journey, and when the two men came back to Jerusalem, they stepped into one of the most important events in the history of the church. The Jerusalem Council met to debate the basis of salvation: Would Gentiles be required to first convert to Judaism when they wanted to become

Christians? James, the leader of the church, listened to both sides and issued his answer: No, Gentiles who trusted in Jesus were full members of the body of Christ. Grace was all they needed. He only asked them to avoid behavior that would deeply offend the Jewish believers.

This issue could have thrown a wet blanket on the growth of the church, but James's opinion opened wide the door of evangelism. Paul asked Barnabas to travel with him to the towns in central Turkey where they'd gone on their first trip. They wanted to encourage and strengthen the fledgling bodies of believers. When Barnabas told Paul he wanted to take John Mark with them again, Paul would have nothing of it. Luke tells us, "They had such a sharp disagreement that they parted company. Barnabas took Mark and sailed for Cyprus, but Paul chose Silas and left, commended by the believers to the grace of the Lord. He went through Syria and Cilicia, strengthening the churches" (Acts 15:39–41).

This was a crucial spiritual event that was recorded in just three verses, and I want to draw your attention to what was happening. Barnabas, the "son of encouragement," was known for his generous heart and incredible character. He was the most influential person in Paul's life (besides Jesus). He is the one person who shows up over and over in the moments that shaped Paul. At first, he put his life on the line to go and meet Paul when none of the other apostles or leaders in Jerusalem would get near him. Later, he had such respect for Paul that he was willing to pursue him and welcome him to share leadership with him over the church at Antioch. Barnabas was the person who stuck with him on the first missionary journey, even when their lives were threatened.

But now Barnabas is standing with the same resolve as he demonstrated in his relationship with Paul, but this time, he gave the benefit of the doubt on behalf of John Mark. This moment makes me stop and reflect on how deep this encounter really was. I'm struck that at this moment, Paul was unwilling to take a chance on John Mark. It doesn't say the Holy Spirit prompted him or impressed upon him that it would be a mistake. It just says he wouldn't consider it.

So, Barnabas walked away with John Mark. I see this as Barnabas living out his convictions as an encourager, no matter who needed his support. In this case, he was unwilling to abandon John Mark because of his mistake. We don't hear anything about what happened to them after they left Paul and Silas, but we can assume that Barnabas protected him from becoming a disgruntled leader, never to be heard of again. Barnabas committed himself to John Mark's success even in the storm. This won't be the last we hear of John Mark.

God used even this moment of disagreement between leaders for good. Instead of one set of missionaries, there were two. Barnabas and John Mark went to Cyprus, and Paul chose Silas to be his companion on the journey to visit the churches he and Barnabas had planted. Still, it's disconcerting that two men of God—one called "the son of encouragement" and the other who taught most powerfully about God's grace and forgiveness—had such a conflict that it drove them apart.

> *"God knows our situation; He will not judge us as if we had no difficulties to overcome. What matters is the sincerity and perseverance of our will to overcome them."*[41]
> —C.S. Lewis

41 C.S. Lewis, *Mere Christianity* (United States: William Collins, 2017), 50.

NEVER SAW IT COMING

I've walked with people through a vast array of struggles. Sometimes they were diligently and faithfully serving God, and they suffered spiritual attacks. Sometimes they were blindsided by a problem they hadn't anticipated. And sometimes, the nagging pressures of life eroded their passion for Christ and His work. After many years of caring for people, I'm not surprised very often, but I had an experience that I never saw coming.

On the first Sunday in January 2018, our church was packed in the first service. I preached on the Prodigal Son. When the second service started, the room was just as full. I got up to speak, and I said, "Turn with me to Luke 15." About five minutes into my message, I started over from the beginning as I told the crowd, "Turn with me to Luke 15." Cheryl and other leaders thought it was odd that I repeated myself, but they assumed it was just a one-off. I preach without notes, so they guessed I'd just mentally lost my place.

However, a lady in the second row went over to Cheryl and whispered, "Steve is having a stroke. You need to do something!"

I wasn't slurring words or experiencing any facial changes, but again, after another five minutes of my message, I told the audience, "Let's turn to Luke 15."

Soon after, I noticed several people getting up and walking in the audience. I wanted to tell them, "Hey, don't you know it takes a lot of concentration to give a talk like this? Please sit down and pay attention!" But of course, I didn't say that.

For a fourth time, I started over by saying, "Please turn with me to Luke 15."

At that point, Larry, our executive pastor, and Cheryl were determining how to intervene and help me. It was as if I was a skipping record. They decided that if it happened again, they would come on stage and help escort me out the back.

Right on cue, I confidently told the people, "Take your Bible and turn to Luke 15."

Nobody knew how I'd respond to someone coming onto the stage and asking me to walk off with him, but there was no other option. In full view of all the people, Larry walked up to me. I had no clue what was happening because nothing like this had ever happened before! He said calmly, "Steve, you're having a medical emergency, and you need to go with Cheryl."

I didn't argue. I just responded, "Okay." Cheryl took me by the hand, and the two of us walked to the side of the stage. The people who had gotten up during my message were doctors and EMTs who were waiting for me behind the curtain. They all said I needed to get to the hospital right away. They debated about the best means of transportation, but Cheryl insisted on driving me. The hospital is only a minute or two from the church.

The ER doctor examined me, and soon, I was admitted to the hospital. They began to administer all of the stroke protocol practices for early intervention, yet nothing could confirm that I had a stroke. Larry came to see me, and I greeted him like I hadn't seen him in a while. A few minutes later, I got distracted talking to the nurse, and when I looked up again, I saw Larry. I exclaimed, "Hey, look. Larry's here!" I had no idea I'd talked to him just moments before.

The doctors conducted a battery of tests, including an MRI and later a test to try to stimulate a seizure. Actually, when they were taking me to have the MRI, I barely realized what was happening. I told the technician, "I can't have an MRI. I have a titanium bone in my inner ear." He didn't know if I was delirious or accurate, so he went out to ask Cheryl about it. She confirmed that I did, in fact, have a piece of metal in my head, which would have been a disaster if they'd gone through with the MRI. Even in my diminished state, God was looking out for me!

All the tests that first afternoon were negative, so one of the doctors said, "We have one more. Tomorrow we'll do a cognitive test." Overnight, I felt better, and it seemed that my mind was clearer. That next day the technician began by giving me five words and asking me to repeat them—piece of cake. For the next thirty minutes or so, she asked me questions, had me draw a number of things, and asked me to count down from one hundred by sevens. I passed with flying colors. Then she said, "Pastor Jamison, what were the five words I asked you to repeat at the beginning of our meeting?" I couldn't remember a single one. A sense of panic enveloped me, and I began to sweat down the sides of my hospital gown. I prayed under my breath, "Lord, help me!" Out of the depths of my foggy mind, one of the words came back, then another, and finally, all five.

The test confirmed what they suspected from the start. I was experiencing a rare condition called *transient global amnesia*. Transient because it comes and goes, global because it affects all short-term memories, and amnesia because I couldn't remember what happened only minutes before. The doctors assured me (and especially Cheryl) that it wasn't dangerous, and it was unlikely to ever happen again.

The neurologist told Cheryl and me, "I'm releasing you from the hospital. Go home and live your life. You're fine."

I couldn't quite grasp what he was saying, so I asked, "Do I need to take a few months off to rest?"

"No," he gently insisted. "You can resume your normal schedule."

I certainly didn't expect that! I said, "I'm supposed to travel overseas in a couple of weeks. You don't think I should go, do you?"

He smiled and repeated, "We've tested you. You're healthy, and it almost certainly won't happen again. Don't worry about this ever again. Live your life."

The doctor's assurance allowed Cheryl to take a deep breath. Suddenly all the pent-up fear and emotions of the previous couple of days flooded her mind and heart. We found ourselves holding each other close and drawing strength from God and each other. The Lord walked us through a time of growing even closer and more grateful for God's loving grace.

When Cheryl and I walked out the back door of our church on that Sunday morning, people in our church wondered if I would ever be back as their pastor. What would the future hold for us personally and for our church? This was one of the most profound moments as our church poured their love and prayers over us and our family. We experienced the bond of God's sacred trust between us and our people in a way few people ever know.

We all know there is nothing more valuable than the love of your family, but I can say that as I faced the storm in the ER, struggling to understand what was happening to me, it was the love of my family that filled my heart in ways that are impossible to express with words. My younger son Jordan was in town. He came into the ER and shared his hug and expression of love. It went deep. My oldest son Josh and his wife, Carrie, aren't only family, they're key leaders in our church. They had started to drive out of town for an event when friends called to tell them, "Hey, something's wrong with your Dad." They turned around and came to the ER. They were so patient and loving with me as I struggled to figure out what was wrong with me ... and feared what this might mean to all of us. Janelle and Brandon reached out from California, expressing how much they loved us and wished they could be with us. Cheryl has been the most amazing wife through our years together. In this dramatic time, she was with me every moment, pouring her love and prayers over me, never leaving my room. I can't say enough about what a gift she is to me. Thank God that He carried us through one of the most significant storms of our lives. The storm wasn't absent of fear, but it was filled with God's presence and comfort in the middle of our crises. Today, I'm grateful to say that I've walked in excellent health with no reoccurrence of amnesia.

A DISASTER WAITING TO HAPPEN

Earlier, I mentioned the difficulty we had when we planned to build a new twenty-acre ministry campus. As you recall, King County has very strict building codes. The process of obtaining a building permit for a major project can take up to seven years. Once approved for a conditional building permit, the project must be completed within five years. We desperately needed a larger building because we had four services every week, and our team was wearing thin.

We had real estate professionals looking high and low for a property where we could build a sizable building. For a long time, the largest parcel they could find was three acres, which was totally inadequate. After an exhausting search, the Lord led us to a twenty-acre site very near to our church. It seemed like a miracle, but there were strings attached. The county hadn't allowed anyone to build on it because there was a shortage of water in the area. They said we'd have to put our name in a lottery, and if we didn't win, we couldn't build. In fact, they said that to have an adequate supply of water for a large church, we'd have to win the lottery twice. (The term "fat chance" may have been uttered.)

As we explored the property, we discovered that the house on it had a commercial water main already connected and no one to this day can explain how or why that happened. We were in business!

We had the option to deliver a preliminary plan to the county building commission, but we decided to complete our plans before we submitted them. Soon after this, the county passed The Critical Areas Ordinance, which limited any newly completed plans to the development of thirty-five percent of the available acreage. A member of the building commission told us that we could build a feed store or veterinary clinic or something comparable, but not a large church. We'd already submitted a completed plan, but the commissioner said that didn't matter because it hadn't been officially approved. We were stuck again.

We hired an attorney who had pled cases before the state Supreme Court. He spent weeks analyzing our plans and the ordinance, talking to county officials, and considering the alternatives. When he finished, he came to our board meeting to make his presentation. He told us, in effect, "You've worked hard, you've been diligent, but the county has you over a barrel, and it's time to fold the tent and go somewhere else. If you're willing to reduce the size of your building, you can build it here. If not, you can't. I'm sorry, but that's how I see it."

It was a very heavy moment. Everyone was silent, and then one of the board members asked, "Pastor Steve, what do you think we should do?"

Instantly I thought, *Who am I to argue with this skilled attorney?* But instead, I said, "The Critical Areas Ordinance looks more like intent than an actual law. We're being pressured. I think we should challenge it. We'll either win big or lose big."

I knew I was out on a limb, so I wasn't sure what to expect from the members of our board. In a few seconds, one of them spoke up, "That rings true to me. We *cannot* cave in. We need to stand strong." The rest of the people around the table agreed. We were going to trust God and fight as one for our church.

When a storm strikes, leaders don't have time to stop and build a culture of mutual trust. It's either there, or it's not. We can be certain that storms will come. We may not know the source or be able to anticipate the intensity, but they'll happen. We need to avoid coasting and making assumptions that getting along well enough is good enough. When the storm rages, we need to be prepared by having a team that operates with a bond of unity, trust, and strength.

But there's more: the Holy Spirit gave us wisdom about how to move forward. It wasn't in fighting the legal issues, but instead, to research and prepare for a meeting with the County Executive. We put together a packet that showed the number of new business licenses that had been issued in the past five years and the square footage of buildings permitted for schools, police, fire and city hall. We plotted the population growth of the county and presented graphs of our church growth. We took an aerial photo and watermarked it, so every page of the report showed the density of the area.

Our lawyer then set up a meeting with our County Executive. In his office, we presented our research and asked just one question, "Why is there room for every part of our community to grow except the church?" It was an amazing meeting. The tide turned by the grace of God, and our building was soon approved.

Today, our church has a beautiful building and an amazing ministry tool. When I look at it, I recall the storm that threatened to sink us, but I also recall the persevering faith of every person on our board. Together, we faced the wind and waves, risking it all for what matters the most, reaching this generation for Christ.

In John's Gospel, Jesus promised the Holy Spirit would come to each believer after He ascended to the Father. The word is sometimes translated as "Comforter" or "Counselor," but maybe a more accurate term is "Advocate." The Holy Spirit is our attorney, the one who represents us, stands up for us, and defends us. He has infinite wisdom and power. In ministry, business, and family relationships, we often operate in our own wisdom and power . . . which are decidedly not infinite! We function best when we're surrendered to the Father's will, trusting in Jesus's blood for forgiveness, and depending on the Spirit's power to accomplish what only He can do.

Years ago, when we fished off the coast of Alaska, we often spent hours peering through binoculars, trying to find a buoy marking the end of our longline. Sometimes, the leaden skies and the sea are almost the same color. I call it "the blur of gray." When GPS became available, we could quickly get within fifty feet of our gear. This contrast is a metaphor of our moral world. We're living in a culture that can't determine right from wrong, blessings from curses—it's the blur of moral gray. But the Holy Spirit gives us direction, warnings, and encouragement to stay on track with God's heart, His will, and His purposes. The Spirit comforts us, counsels us, and acts as our advocate. We never face these storms alone. Don't leave home without Him.

STORIES OF RESILIENCE

I've had the privilege of getting to know some remarkable people who have trusted God when things looked very dark. As you read their stories, put yourself in their shoes and imagine living with their persevering faith.

HOPE IN THE STORM

Luke Ridnour played high school basketball for his Dad in Blaine, Washington, and then went on to star at the University of Oregon. He was named PAC 10 Player of the Year and was chosen by the Seattle Sonics in the first round of the NBA draft. Luke had a dream come true to play for the home team and have friends and family in the stands.

Luke and his wife, Kate, were both college athletes. They married after Luke joined the Sonics, and they would later have their first baby. The future was looking bright, but then things became difficult. The team was sold and moved to another city, Luke was traded, and then, when Kate was pregnant with twins, they received the devastating news that the twins had serious health problems. The medical team recommended they consider ending the pregnancy. Though Luke and Kate were facing the storm of their lives, they knew there was only one answer for them: to batten down the hatches and trust God to bring them through.

This storm didn't catch God off guard. Prior to Kate's pregnancy with the twins, Luke had verbally committed to the Los Angeles Lakers. They were excited to have a run for an NBA title in LA, but the deal fell through, and Luke ended up signing with the Minnesota Timberwolves, the worst team in the league. Luke and Kate asked God for a supernatural miracle of healing, but the answer didn't happen exactly as they had hoped. When the boys were born, one of them had a very rare condition called esophageal atresia, where the esophagus isn't connected to the stomach. But God knew what Luke and Kate needed more than they did. The world's only surgeon who specializes in this rare surgical procedure was at Children's Hospital in Minneapolis, Minnesota. Children are flown in from around the world to have surgery there. God had positioned Luke and Kate for the very best medical help for their son.

It was a tremendously difficult time for Luke and Kate as they tried to balance the needed surgeries for their son and the demands of playing in the NBA. But as they leaned into the Lord and filled their lives with worship and God's Word, the Lord stood near. Today the twins are the joy of the family, bringing smiles and lots of laughs.

Luke left the NBA a few years ago, and the family moved back to their hometown of Blaine, Washington. Recently, Kate delivered their sixth child—all boys. They announced the sixth child by taking a picture of five boys wearing basketball jerseys with Ridnour across the top of the back and numbered one through five, with another jersey with the number six draped over a chair next to them.

Today Luke and Kate minister to their small, tight-knit community through youth basketball. They've hosted worship nights for the community and share the faith that God forged in them through a difficult time. They stand as a great source of strength for many other parents facing similar storms of life.

ONLY GOD

A few years ago, Karen Wright was doing what she did every school day, dropping her kids off before the first bell rang. There in the parking lot, she had a pulmonary embolism, a ruptured blood vessel in her lung. Paramedics resuscitated her and rushed her to the hospital. I arrived as a family member walked through the ER door. The doctors told us, "We have her on a ventilator so she can breathe, but I'm sorry to tell you that there's no brain activity. The situation is hopeless." I asked if there was any possibility she could live, and the doctor shook his head, "If she survives, her brain injuries are so severe that she'll never be conscious."

Normally, I'd have been resigned to what seemed inevitable, but I'd known a man who had a severe heart attack, and his heart was stopped for about twenty-five minutes. The doctors told his mother that his brain had been without oxygen for much too long, and he showed no brain activity. She was a praying woman, and when she heard this devastating report, she said simply, "He'll be up in three days." She was wrong. It took five days, but suddenly,

168

he opened his eyes and God began to restore his life. It was truly a miracle of God.

With this faith reminder, I turned to her family and said, "Let's just put Karen in God's hands and see what He does." We anointed her with oil and prayed for her recovery. Nothing happened, but our church and her family continued to ask God for a miracle. Time passed, then an EEG showed a blip of activity, then later, more and more. After a few days, Karen was awake and she was restored completely back to normal. Today, she is a beam of hope with a brilliant smile and a heart of gratitude knowing that God spared her life for a purpose.

WAKE-UP CALL

Bob Mortimer and his brother never met a party they didn't like. Late at night after one of these binges, they were both drunk on their way home on a windswept road. Bob was passed out as his brother drove. But his brother couldn't stay awake—the car careened off the road, went over an embankment, and came to rest at the bottom of a hill. The roof was collapsed, but they both survived and were able to climb out of the car. On this dark night, they laughed that the headlights were still on. For some reason, they decided to race up the hill to the road to flag down a ride home. Bob won the race, but when he stepped onto the road, he didn't see a powerline the car had clipped on the plunge. About 12,500 volts raced through Bob's body and blew his kneecaps through his jeans. When he dropped to the ground, he fell on three more lines, burning his clothes to his body.

Somehow, Bob was still alive. As his brother held his bleeding body, a car cautiously stopped to offer assistance. Bob was flown to Harborview Hospital in Seattle, with the best trauma center in the area.

Bob went through a long and difficult recovery, as both legs and one of his arms had to be amputated. He was deeply depressed, and to numb his physical and emotional pain, he turned again to drugs and alcohol. A friend had invited him to church many times, but he refused again and again. Finally, he gave in. There, he encountered God's redemptive love and a hope he'd never known before. Bob gave his heart to Christ and was soon baptized in water.

The story doesn't end there, however. Bob met a beautiful young woman, Darla, they were married, and today, they have three adult children. Bob traveled with me for seven years across the country as we spoke in public schools to help students find hope and healing. Today Bob continues to travel and speak to diverse groups such as the cadets at West Point and soldiers at Walter Reed Medical Center, as well as schools and churches. If you meet Bob, you'll be amazed at his sense of humor and infectious joy. He's a dear friend and an inspiration to all who meet him. He lives every day with gratitude for God's miraculous gift of grace, hope, and love.

WHEN WATERS RUSH IN

Sometimes, we can see the storms coming. Health problems accelerate, an adult child keeps making bad decisions, unresolved conflict causes more resentment, and pressures multiply. But from time to time, they break over us like a huge wave crashing on the deck of my Dad's boat, and we find ourselves in the thick of the storm wearing only our underwear! Let me offer some advice to help you persevere:

PAY ATTENTION TO THE WARNING SIGNS

Don't stick your head in the sand when you see a downward trend in any aspect of your life and relationships. Road signs give us vital information to turn this way or that, to speed up or slow down. Notice and do something about it when your credit card debt keeps growing, when you feel lethargic when a valued relationship has gone sour, when you feel that your life doesn't matter, or you see any other road sign that demands your attention.

Learn more about the role of the Holy Spirit in your life. There's a commercial that says, "If you've got it, a truck brought it." We could paraphrase it to say, "If something good is happening in your life, the Holy Spirit is the source." Some people don't think of the Holy Spirit at all, and others focus primarily on the more dramatic actions of the Spirit. We need to realize that He illuminates the Scriptures so we grasp what God wants to say to us, He affirms the fact that we're God's dear children, He whispers and nudges to move us in the direction we need to go, He empowers us to be effective in giving and serving, and He puts us in touch with the heart of God. If any of this is new to you, take time to read and learn more about the Spirit's presence, power, and purpose in your life.

PRAY PAUL'S PRAYERS

One of the ways we can keep in step with the Spirit is to pray along with Paul. We find his prayers for the churches in two places in Ephesians (Chapters 1 and 3) and in the first chapters of Colossians and Philippians. We can be sure we're in tune with God's heart when we take time to meditate on these prayers and make them our own. And if you need to grow in perseverance, you can be sure that God will answer these prayers authored by the one who endured suffering wherever he went as he was led by the Spirit.

REMEMBER JESUS

Jesus told us, "Follow Me." Where does He lead? Sometimes into great blessings, and sometimes through heartache and pain. He endured so that we might have hope. When we look to Him, we realize that He had a purpose that transcended His pain, and that purpose was rescuing you and me.

LOOK FOR THE SOMETHING SOLID AND GRAB ON TIGHT

In storms off the coast of Alaska, sometimes the best we could do was hang on, so we grabbed anything that was fixed and stable. Jesus is our anchor, our rock, our fortress. In your storms, grab hold of Him and never let go.

STORMS ARE INEVITABLE

We can avoid some of them, but not all of them. They may be caused by our own mistakes and sins, the mistakes and sins of others, natural disasters, and other factors that are out of our control. And if we're in the middle of God's will, at least some of the difficulties we face will be caused by the enemy of our souls, the one who wants to stop us at all cost.

*"Never allow a storm to make you
question the presence of God."*[42]
—Craig Groeschel

Learn about the ministries of Eastridge Church.

---

42 Craig Groeschel, *God with US: Week 3 - Storm with Craig Groeschel*. YouTube (2017, December 19), Retrieved March 9, 2023, from https://www.youtube.com/watch?v=zZETKKhQ2Yg&t=370s

CHAPTER 8

BAIT IN THE WATER

"It's not what you get, but what you give that is God's true measure of a life."[43]
—ELIZABETH GEORGE

he most important and dangerous part of the fishing trip is setting the gear. As I've described before, it involves launching anchors, buoy bags, and radar reflective poles to start the process, and then miles of gear and thousands of baited hooks that shoot off the stern into the ocean. Some days the seas are beautifully calm, but most of the time, the boat is bucking into the wind and the seas as the gear is being launched. While all of that is happening, the main line, called the "ground line," is spinning off of a reel. The gear is going over the stern while the baited hooks are flying by. It's dangerous in so many ways, because a hook could catch a hand, a glove, or an eye.

One day in rough conditions, we were setting our longline when another boat suddenly appeared amid the huge waves. It

43 Elizabeth George, *Walking With the Women of the Bible: A Devotional Journey Through God's Word* (Eugene, Oregon: Harvest House Publishers, 2008)

had been hidden from the radar by the size of the waves. Dad had to slow down to keep from hitting it. As the boat passed by dangerously close, we all held our breath, knowing they were blowing their gear out right across our bow. Their line and hooks were sinking as our boat went over them. Suddenly, their gear hung up on our two stabilizers. (These are weighted plates of steel and concrete designed to moderate the roll of the boat in heavy seas. Each stabilizer is lowered from the rigging on either side of the boat and dragged thirty to forty feet below the surface.)

Seconds later, the stabilizers flew out of the water just above the stern. They were caught up and sliding on the other boat's gear, and they came together and crashed into each other behind our boat. Our boat rolled to port and then starboard, and each time, the heavy stabilizers collided. If they came onto the back of the boat, one of us could be in serious trouble.

At that instant, Dad yelled at me to cut the other boat's gear free. I quickly grabbed a large bait knife and crawled to the stern. As I held the knife and the boat rolled, I realized I had to time my cut perfectly because the stabilizers were only a few feet above my head. If I timed it wrong, my arm ... or my body ... could be crushed. I whispered a prayer for God to help me, and I paused for a second. I was going to move the next time the plates collided.

At the precise moment, I jumped up to cut the line. The tension was so powerful that when I cut it, the gear went flying in opposite directions. It had been dangerous, but it had worked. The crisis was over for both boats. The damaged gear on the bottom could be recovered, and the stabilizers fell back in place. I'll never forget that minute and a half of sheer adrenaline.

Launching the gear is the key to the entire trip. Every farmer knows you need seed in the field to have a harvest and every fisherman knows you need baited hooks to catch fish. This is a practical reality but also a spiritual principle.

> *"The law of harvest is to reap more than you sow. Sow an act, and you reap a habit; sow a habit, and you reap a character; sow a character and you reap a destiny."*[44]
> —G.D. Broadman

THE BEST BAIT

My Dad invested a lot of money in the very best bait. Many of the other crews used primarily herring, but Dad bought salmon and octopus, which halibut prefer over any other kind of food. He bought some herring in case we ran out of the better bait, but we only used herring as a last resort. Dad's priority was always to use the very best. Some other captains and their crews thought he was crazy to spend so much money on salmon and octopus—those guys planned to eat them, not put them on hooks!

Dad's expensive preparation always paid off. We usually returned with the fish hold filled to the brim with halibut, while many other boats returned only half full. Dad's investment in the very best preparation proved over and over again to be a brilliant business move. But it was more than a business move, he was living out the principles of the Bible—you must sow in order to reap.

---

44 Julia Hoitt, *Excellent Quotations for Home and School, Classic Reprint* (United States: Fb&c Limited, 2018), 76.

We can all agree that traveling to Alaska and choosing to drop miles of empty hooks on the bottom of the ocean would be a complete waste of time, expense, and labor. It's nearly the same amount of work to put out empty hooks as baited ones, but with no hope of a return. Who would do that? Yet, this is how many of us operate in our walk with God. We miss the plans and opportunities God has for us to thrive, to grow, and to bear the fruit of the kingdom in our lives. When we fail to honor God as the Bible teaches with tithing and giving, we're basically laying down empty hooks but expecting God's blessing. In this chapter we are going to focus on the keys to never dropping an empty hook and never missing the blessing God intends for your life.

Wise and generous stewardship never goes to waste. Jesus spoke about the importance of the kingdom of God and living as a steward. In sharing the parable of the talents, Jesus spoke of how God expects us to bring a return on what He has entrusted to us. (See Matthew 25:14–30.) And in Psalm 24:1-2, we are taught that everything in the earth is the Lord's. He is the owner; we are stewards of His gifts.

This is how many of us operate in our walk with God. We miss the plans and opportunities God has for us to thrive, to grow, and to bear the fruit of the kingdom in our lives.

MY FIRST LESSON IN GIVING

Fishing for halibut and fishing for tuna aren't similar at all. When we dropped longlines for halibut in the early spring, it was usually cold and stormy. We cut bait, baited the hooks, and put out miles of gear. We worked shifts of twenty-hour days because the boat never slept—the crew was always working really hard. When we brought the lines in and unhooked the halibut, we had to dress each one before icing them below the deck. Later in the season, in the middle of summer, we moved down the coast to find tuna. They travel in schools, and when we were in them, the action was fast and furious. We fished with two huge poles that were part of the boat's rigging system. You may have seen a "troller" using these poles laying out one on each side of the boat with various lengths of lines that we used to fish jigs. Shorter lines were also placed to fish right off the stern, and when we were in a school, we pulled in one after the other. We quickly dropped each one in a brine tank, and then they were flash-frozen. As I've mentioned, tuna don't bite after sundown, so we could relax and get some sleep. We'd wake up the next morning and do it all over again. Basically, tuna fishing was a long, challenging boat ride.

We often went tuna fishing for three weeks between 200 and 1,000 miles offshore, but on one trip, we didn't see land for forty days all the way to Hawaii. We didn't make port there. We fished about three hundred miles off the northern side of the islands, filled the hold and came back home. When I told this story to a friend, he was amazed and asked, "You had enough diesel fuel for a trip like that?"

I explained that we put fuel bladders in the hold where we would later store fish. As the trip continued, we took bladders out to fill our fuel tanks, which gave more room for the fish we were catching. This system worked really well.

Occasionally, we had a slow day when we couldn't find a school. On one of these days, when I was fourteen, I was sitting in the galley as my Dad walked in. He looked over at me and noticed I had a legal pad and I was writing a list of numbers. He asked, "Son, what are you up to?"

I told him, "Not much. I'm just figuring out my crew share."

By this time, I'd added up all the numbers and circled the total at the bottom of the page. Dad leaned over, took a long look at my figures, and said, "You made a mistake."

I argued, "No, I don't think so." I pointed to each number and explained, "This is the weight of fish on board, this is the current market price, here are the expenses, and this is my share of the profits." I was sure I was right.

Dad motioned for me to hand him my pencil. Under my final total, he deducted ten percent and wrote down a new total. He looked at me and smiled, "Steve, ten percent is God's crew share, not yours. Don't ever confuse the two." He was teaching me that God desires a real relationship with us and that we need to respond with love and honor to God.

YOUR GREATEST HARVEST

When discussing stewardship and generosity, we usually focus on three aspects: our time, talents, and treasure. These three areas, of course, are crucial building blocks of a life that honors God, but I believe there's one more that's just as important: our testimony. We need to be good stewards of our stories of faith, how God miraculously saved us (and every salvation is a miracle of making dead people alive!), and of the way He has moved in our lives and our families to shine His light in our darkness.

Our stories of finding Christ (or more accurately, Christ finding us) describe our greatest treasure. We were without hope, but God rescued us. We were helpless, but God provided what we needed. We often felt worthless, but in Christ, we're sons and daughters of the King! Some of us have thought about how to tell others about our salvation experience, but many have assumed, "That's the pastor's job, not mine." But we all have the privilege of speaking the Good News to those who are perishing.

Some people, even those who have been in church for many years, can't imagine telling anyone about Jesus. They may assume they don't know enough to be clear and accurate, or they may be afraid of the person's response. Whatever the reason, let me put at least some of your fears to rest. We all love to hear great stories, and we love to tell them. That's all evangelism is: telling your story of what Jesus has done for you. You don't need three hours to go through the entire book of Romans with someone. In fact, you can tell your story in only a couple of minutes—and God may use you to change the destiny of eternity for that person!

We were without hope, but God rescued us. We were helpless, but God provided what we needed. We often felt worthless, but in Christ, we're sons and daughters of the King!

Here are three quick steps that will give you clarity and confidence as you to share your faith. When you understand these three simple steps, the Holy Spirit can lead you to share them in as little as two minutes, but of course, you may have the opportunity to take more time.

- First, ask for permission to tell your story. You can say something like, "Would you mind if I tell you about a relationship that means a lot to me?" Start here by sharing what was going on in your life before you met Christ. Some people assume they need to have a horrific life story for this part to be meaningful, but that's not the case. Most people can relate to a story of emptiness, misplaced priorities, strained relationships, or family background.

- Second, share what brought you to the awareness of your need for Jesus in your life (How did the lights go on for you about Jesus?). Most people are wide open to hearing an authentic story of what led you to trust Jesus. Describe the moment, any hesitation, and the decision.

- And third, talk about the changes God has made in your life. How have you found peace, pardon, and purpose?

I don't advise sharing a lot of Scripture in the first conversation, but pick one about Christ's sacrifice that's most meaningful to you. I often use Romans 5:8, Romans 6:23, and of course, John 3:16.

Sharing your story is a spiritual experience. Trust the Spirit to lead you to the right person at the right time, and trust Him to open the person's heart to the message of the gospel of grace. Most people need several conversations before they understand that Christ accepts us based on what He has done for us, not what we do for Him. The first conversation is just a starting point. You don't need to press the person for a decision—that's the Holy Spirit's job! Just share the love of Jesus and watch Him work.

PRAY FOR OPPORTUNITIES

The best coaching I can give you is to pray every day for God to give you open doors. This will transform how you see your life and how you interact with people. Two things happen when you join God's most important work of reaching people for Christ. First, the Lord will see your heart and start bringing spiritually hungry people across your path. Secondly, the Holy Spirit will prompt you in the moment to show you when a door is opening so you can step in to share your heart. Prayer and expectation make the difference between seeing opportunities as they open or walking away thinking, *That would have been a great moment to have shared what Christ has done in my life!*

A great example of this happened on a Monday Night Football broadcast. On January 2, 2023, during a Monday Night NFL football game, Buffalo Bills defensive safety Damar Hamlin tackled Cincinnati Bengal's wide receiver, Tee Higgins. Damar stood up after the tackle, and seconds later, he suffered a full cardiac arrest and fell to the ground. Medical staff from both teams went to work to try and save his life. The players from both teams were on their knees, praying and calling out to God. ESPN analyst Dan Orlovsky was on "NFL Live" when he said, "Maybe this is not the right thing to do, but it's on my mind to pray for Damar Hamlin right now." He told the national audience, "I'm going do it out loud; I'm going close my eyes. I'm going to bow my head, and I'm just going pray for him."[45] Everyone on the set bowed their heads and prayed as well. Immediately, people posted the scene on social media, and it went viral, calling millions of people around the world to pray. Weeks later, when Damar Hamlin attended the Super Bowl, he gave thanks to God and to all who prayed for him.

Orlovsky didn't share his testimony, and he didn't make a classic gospel presentation, but in a powerful way, he pointed millions of people to Jesus. He could easily have just narrated the scene on the field, but he saw an opportunity to represent the love and power of Jesus. Sometimes the greatest open door can come by just asking someone if there is something you can pray with them about.

Barry Meguiar is a tremendous businessman (Meguiar's Car Wax) and a great example of a person being on mission every day in the marketplace. Barry makes it his mission to seek an opportunity to share with people the goodness of God. He's a master at allowing God to open doors of opportunity. Check out this QR code where you can hear more of his story and testimony.

Learn more about Barry Meguiar.

45 Sports Spectrum. (2023, January 2), *ESPN's Dan Orlovsky Praying for Damar Hamlin on NFL Live*, YouTube. https://www.youtube.com/watch?v=J1Vs59RDITc

One of the greatest gifts that God can place in our lives is the sense of being led to the things that matter the most.

Why don't we share our testimonies more often and more clearly? There may be several reasons: We're not prepared, we don't believe people will listen, our hearts have grown cold toward God, and we're afraid we'll look foolish if we open our mouths to talk about Jesus. In Peter's first letter, he gives us clear directions, not only about the content of our message but also our motive and tone: "But in your hearts revere Christ as Lord. Always be prepared to give an answer to everyone who asks you to give the reason for the hope that you have. But do this with gentleness and respect, keeping a clear conscience, so that those who speak maliciously against your good behavior in Christ may be ashamed of their slander" (1 Peter 3:15-16). Peter is saying: Always be ready. You never know when you may have a divine appointment with someone who needs Jesus. You're imparting hope; everyone is searching for something or someone that gives them hope, but true hope is found only in the love of God. You don't need to browbeat people or argue with them to make them believe. Just share your story with kindness and care, and let the Spirit do His work to open the person's heart to believe. And make sure your conduct matches your words. People of integrity have already earned the right to be heard, even if the hearer doesn't agree with the message.

The Holy Spirit will also help you see how you can be most effective in life, business, and ministry. One of the greatest gifts that God can place in our lives is the sense of being led to the things that matter the most. When we begin to live with a kingdom heart, God can bless our talents, treasure, time, and testimony in remarkable ways. You can live with purpose and an anointing focused on the most valuable catch every day.

> *"When you live your life for God's glory,*
> *everything you do can become worship."*[46]
> —Rick Warren

THE SPIRIT'S "NO" AND "YES"

Remember that the Holy Spirit is active in you and the other person when you share your testimony. When Paul and Silas traveled to central Turkey to encourage the churches planted on the first journey, they met Timothy in Lystra, the city where the crowd believed Paul and Barnabas were gods . . . until they changed their minds and stoned Paul! Timothy had a good reputation among the believers, so Paul invited him to join them.

The following scenes show how the Spirit directed the three companions. They traveled through Phrygia and Galatia, in the center of Turkey, "having been kept by the Holy Spirit from preaching the word in the province of Asia" (Acts 16:6), which includes the major port city of Ephesus. They planned to go north to Bithynia, which borders on the Black Sea, "but the Spirit of

---

46 Rick Warren, *The Purpose Driven Life: What on Earth Am I Here For?* (Philippines: Zondervan, 2003), 56.

Jesus [another term for the Holy Spirit] would not allow them to" (v.7). They passed by Mysia and traveled to the northwest coastal city of Troas (ancient Troy). I can imagine the three men wondered why in the world the Spirit had led them on a detour of 400 miles without letting them stop to plant churches along the way. The answer was soon to come:

> *During the night, Paul had a vision of a man from Macedonia standing and begging him, "Come over to Macedonia and help us." After Paul had seen the vision, we got ready at once to leave for Macedonia, concluding that God had called us to preach the gospel to them. —vv. 9-10*

Macedonia is in Europe: The Holy Spirit was opening the door for the gospel to another continent. He had led Paul's small team many miles, and I'm sure they were confused at times, but He had them right where He wanted them. For you and me, the Holy Spirit might open a door for us to talk to a neighbor, a coworker, a friend, or a family member. When we're sensitive to the Spirit's promptings, He'll show us where to put our bait in the water, where the fish are biting, and perhaps where no one has fished before. As we follow His leading, God will give us opportunities to tell people what Jesus has done in our lives.

> *"Success is...knowing your purpose in life, growing to reach your maximum potential, and sowing seeds that benefit others."*[47]
> —John C. Maxwell

---

47 John C. Maxwell, *Your Road Map for Success: You Can Get There from Here* (United States: Thomas Nelson, 2002), 11.

A ONCE IN A LIFETIME FISHING TIP

One of my Dad's closest friends was a man named Pete. He was a top tuna fisherman. Fishermen are some of the most competitive people you will ever meet. Dad and Pete had built a strong friendship during many years of fishing the same waters. One day while in port, Pete shared with my Dad his best secret about catching tuna. He took a clear glass of water and slipped a new piece of monofilament line into the water and it basically disappeared. Then he pull it out and scuffed the line and then put it back in the water. This time where the line was scuffed the light refracted on it and you could see the line in the water. The tuna hit the jig with such speed and force that their teeth leave small frays on the leader. It was a very simple tip: to frequently cut and replace the clear monofilament leader line on the front of the tuna jigs. When we returned to sea, we put his advice to work, and we were stunned to see the immediate impact. In fact, it changed our family income for years to come. Pete's generosity for my dad and our family left an impact that we will never forget. It endeared and deepened an already strong friendship. Just one tip had the power to change our future.

Here is where it gets really good, God has given us the most important tip about walking in his presence and power. The " tip" is simply this, Jesus desires your heart and love above all things. He came to the earth and gave his life to demonstrate his love for us while we were still sinners (Romans 5:8). Everything God speaks in his word is designed to pull you into a deeply meaningful and everlasting relationship with him! If you can grasp this truth of his love, you will never be the same.

God desires to be at the center of your life. He has shown us many forms of worship, but what may be the highest form is honoring God with our tithe and offerings. The moment you read this a spiritual battle may break out. But, I want to take a few moments to explain the reason why God has chosen throughout the Bible to teach us the importance of honoring him through giving.

In this one act of honoring God through generosity, it is amazing what it communicates to God about our heart and love for him. When we give from a heart of worship, we are expressing gratitude, honor, faith, obedience, trust, and love for God's people and His work. In return God promises to meet our needs, he changes our heart and plants generosity in us that blesses everyone who shares life with us. God places giving central in our worship to draw us close.

In Paul's second letter to the Corinthians, he encouraged them to give generously to relieve the famine devastating the people in Palestine.

Remember this: Whoever sows sparingly will also reap sparingly, and whoever sows generously will also reap generously. Each of you should give what you have decided in your heart to give, not reluctantly or under compulsion, for God loves a cheerful giver. And God is able to bless you abundantly, so that in all things at all times, having all that you need, you will abound in every good work. As it is written: 'They have freely scattered their gifts to the poor; their righteousness endures forever.' Now he who supplies seed to the sower and bread for food will also supply and increase your store of seed and will enlarge the harvest of your righteousness. You will be enriched in every way so that you can be generous on every occasion, and through us, your generosity will result in thanksgiving to God. —2 Corinthians 9:6–11

Notice that God gives us two things: seed to sow and bread to eat. The bread is for sustenance now; the seed is sown for a harvest that will sustain us later. Far too many believers look for today's bread but they don't invest in planting seeds for tomorrow (they eat the bread and the seed). As you look closer, God gave them a principle and a promise: "Now he who supplies seed to the sower and bread for food will also supply and increase your store of seed and will enlarge the harvest of your righteousness. You will be enriched in every way so that you can be generous on every occasion, and through us, your generosity will result in thanksgiving to God" (2 Corinthians 9:10-11). The principle is that God is generous in giving us what we need today (bread for food) and a harvest to meet tomorrow's needs (seed to the sower). The promise is that God will bless and multiply not only seed and bread but our righteousness. He says there are no limits to the scope of God's blessing. We'll be "enriched in every way," not just financially; "so we can be generous on every occasion," not too narrowly focused; which results "in thanksgiving to God," which acknowledges that everything we are and everything we have are gifts from God.

This scripture is so powerful and brings such meaning to our love and worship to God. The text states that God loves a cheerful giver, remember God is pulling our hearts to him.

The kingdom of God is upside down from the secular world. The principles of the world tell us to get whatever we can and never let go; in God's kingdom, we've already received the greatest gift, and our hearts are full and overflowing. The world focuses on acquisition and hoarding so we can feel safe from need; God's kingdom focuses on giving out of the wealth of time, talent, treasure, and testimony God has already entrusted to us. The world jockeys for greatness, power, and control to dominate others; in God's kingdom, we're humbled by the magnitude of God's grace toward us, so we delight in serving Him and the people around us.

In one of Jesus's most familiar statements, He told the crowd: *"Do not store up for yourselves treasures on earth, where moths and vermin destroy, and where thieves break in and steal. But store up for yourselves treasures in heaven, where moths and vermin do not destroy, and where thieves do not break in and steal. For where your treasure is, there your heart will be also."* —Matthew 6:19–21

For years, I assumed that our treasure followed our heart's desire, but that's not what Jesus is saying. He says that our heart's desire follows what we treasure.

Put another way; our investments dictate the condition of our hearts. I've heard people say that a person can get an accurate picture of his heart by taking a good look at two things: his schedule and his spending.

We have choices every day—and every minute of every day—to invest in the things God values . . . or not. Our use of money isn't the only indicator of the condition of our hearts, but it's a good one. In the last book of the Old Testament, the people and God are in an argument. He accuses them of robbing Him. They're outraged and defensively ask why He would say that. God's answer: He doesn't need anything from them because He's the Creator of the entire universe, but they are withholding what

He's due: tithes and offerings. Even then, God offers a path to correct their flaws so they can be in a place of blessing:

"Bring the whole tithe into the storehouse, that there may be food in my house. Test me in this," says the LORD Almighty, "and see if I will not throw open the floodgates of heaven and pour out so much blessing that there will not be room enough to store it. I will prevent pests from devouring your crops, and the vines in your fields will not drop their fruit before it is ripe," says the LORD Almighty. "Then all the nations will call you blessed, for yours will be a delightful land," says the LORD Almighty.
—Malachi 3:10–12

Many people assume the promised blessing is money, but it's much more than that. Money isn't what really satisfies. I know people who have more money than love, more money than fulfillment, more money than joy, and more money than purpose. In those cases, money promises more than it can deliver. Instead, God promises that the blessing of generosity is a rich life of love, fulfillment, joy, and purpose. He will protect the work of our hands from pests (the enemy's attacks) and frost (unforeseen circumstances). We'll enjoy shalom and genuine peace, and we'll see that our generosity advances the kingdom of God as people notice God's generosity to us.

In the Lord's Prayer, we ask God to give us "our daily bread." When our staff team prays according to this pattern of prayer, we say, "Lord, give us everything we need to do Your will." It's more than today's bread to eat so that we don't die of hunger; it's the Bread of Life who loves us and leads us as we participate with Him in the greatest enterprise the world has ever known: reaching into every corner of our neighborhood and every part of the world with the amazing message of God's love, grace, and power.

We shouldn't be surprised that the story of Barnabas's influence begins with a gift. Generosity is the gateway, the open door to God's shower of blessings. It's how trust is established, and it's how trust grows. It cements relationships and forms the bedrock for risk-taking that can change a community.

You may sense that you need to step into someone's life with a word or a resource. Pay attention to the nudge. If you feel inadequate, overcome your fears by getting some practical help or learning to trust God as you step into the unknown. Do you sense someone saying, "Come help us," like Paul saw in the Macedonian vision? Do you see a need that isn't being met, but you have the resources to meet it?

Generosity isn't primarily about our gifts; it's about God and His kingdom. If we focus on the amount we give, we'll either begrudge every dollar that leaves our bank account, or we'll feel pride that we've been a savior—neither of those is a good motive, and neither of them reinforces a thankful heart. Instead, develop a kingdom mindset, saying, "God, all I have is Yours, and You've given me the unspeakable privilege of being Your partner in expanding the kingdom. Thank you so much."

Loving the Lord and living your life as worship to him and for His glory is what matters the most. As you seek to invest your time, talents, treasure, and testimony in someone else's breakthrough, you will no longer be laying miles of empty hooks on the bottom with no hope of a harvest. All of these investments are like putting the best bait on our hooks. The best bait produces the best catch. You will live a life of vision and passion reaching for kingdom impact.

"The most obvious lesson in Christ's teaching is that there is no happiness in having or getting anything, but only in giving."[48]
—Henry Drummond

AN OBJECT LESSON

We were in the middle of a Jammin' event in Puerto Rico, and my day was a whirlwind of activity. In the middle of it all, our team had lunch in a food court in a mall across the street from the Roberto Clemente Arena. As we talked, I noticed a guy standing near the trash cans. As people dumped their scraps, he intercepted them and asked if he could eat the leftovers. I asked our interpreter if anyone knew this man. It turned out he was a pastor from Cuba visiting one of the leaders on our local team. I wanted to talk with him and see how we could help.

As I introduced myself and asked why he was eating scraps, he explained that he and his family often ate only one meal a day, and he couldn't stand to see this food go to waste. He also told us he was a pastor from Cuba. As he bent down to pick up more leftovers, I noticed that his shoes had holes in them—big holes. The Holy Spirit prompted me to ask him if I could buy him a pair of shoes, but I had very mixed emotions. I had a lot to do that day, and I couldn't afford to waste time on things that weren't crucial to our ministry. We were in a mall, so I quickly looked for the nearest shoe store. My inner clock was ticking. There wasn't one, so my

---

48 *Addresses* by Henry Drummond, 1891, p. 38.

interpreter drove us to a store down the road. By this time, I was calculating the things I was missing as I went on this crazy chase.

We walked into the store, and the pastor picked out a pair of shoes. I told the interpreter to tell him to buy two pairs. A minute or two later, he was beaming when he showed them to me. Then, the Spirit reminded me of my wife's devotion to me and our ministry, and I was sure the man's wife could use a new pair of shoes. Through my interpreter, I asked him if she needed shoes. He reached into his pocket and pulled out a piece of paper with his wife's foot size drawn on it. I told him to pick out two pairs of shoes for her, too. In a few minutes, he had four boxes on the counter.

I told the interpreter to ask if he had children and if they needed shoes. Astoundingly, the man reached into his pocket and pulled out pieces of paper inscribed with outlines of his son's and daughter's feet. Soon, we walked out of the store with eight boxes of shoes. After we put them in the trunk of our car, the man told the interpreter that he wanted to tell me something. He said that he made $11 a month driving a taxi in Cuba. He had been preaching to his church about God's promise to provide for all our needs. One day his daughter asked him, "Daddy if God is going to meet all our needs, why are we hungry? And why do our shoes have holes in them?" He said her questions drove him to his knees.

The Lord spoke to him and directed him to cut out paper outlines of everyone in the family. He said, "When you have the opportunity to preach in Puerto Rico, you will meet a man who will buy shoes for everyone in your family." The day I met him at the food court was his last day before returning to Cuba. He hadn't told anyone about his family's need for shoes or the Lord's promise. He just waited to see how God would meet the need.

That night at the hotel, I got on my knees and thanked God for prompting me to disrupt my day, so I could be His partner in meeting the needs of this dear family. I was stunned and humbled. I had been so wrapped up in my schedule and priorities that I had been concerned about lost time. I felt broken . . . in a good way . . . because God had allowed me to be a part of a tangible demonstration of His love and presence.

Then, the Lord had another word for me: It would have taken months, if not years, for the pastor to save enough money to buy a pair of shoes for his wife and children, but He brought me to help. God showed me that He would do the same thing for me. He was going to bring people who would help me expand the reach of Jammin'.

A short time later, Luis Palau and his son Kevin called me. They'd heard that we were planning an event in Washington, D.C., and they asked if I could use some help. I said, "Yes, that would be great!" So they sent Luis's youngest son, Andrew, to the city to assist in the preparations.

Andrew was a tremendous blessing to me on so many levels. He was a hard worker and was doing everything he could to lay the groundwork for a significant outreach, but on a personal level, he was a friend and a great place of encouragement. One thing that really struck me was Andrew's tenderness to God. Every time we were in a meeting of leaders and he was asked to share his story, he wept all the way through it.

You see, not long before, Andrew had been kicked out of Biola University in California, had moved to Boston, and was far from

God. His parents, Luis and Pat, prayed and believed God to turn their son's life around, and they invited him to join them for an evangelistic crusade in Jamaica. Andrew wasn't interested . . . until they offered to take him deep sea fishing. On this trip, God had prepared a divine appointment. Andrew opened his heart as God poured in His grace, forgiveness, and restorative power.

"The rest of the story" is that in Jamaica, Andrew fell in love with the daughter of a friend of the Palaus, and they were married. Her sister married Toby McKeehan, better known as TobyMac. The streams of God's blessings converged in our Washington outreach when John Jenkins got involved, Andrew became a vital part of our team, and TobyMac performed at the event. Only God could pull all that off.

In Puerto Rico, God's generosity was shown in my "chance encounter" with the poor pastor from Cuba. Pausing my day to care for someone else taught me a valuable lesson in responding to God's prompts. When I look back on how God orchestrated my unexpected relationship with the Cuban pastor, the prompting that God would bring me the help I desperately needed, the Palaus' kindness and generosity to offer their help, and the bond of friendship between Andrew and me, I want to laugh . . . and I want to thank the God who is so magnificently creative and gracious. What a series of gifts!

When we give to our churches and mission organizations, the impact of our generosity is beyond sending missionaries to the field and supporting building and support projects. We're blowing fresh wind into the sails of people who are on the move seeking and serving God. I can imagine the scene when the Cuban pastor walked through the door of his home. He gave them the shoes, of course, but I'm sure he also told them about God prompting him to take papers with outlines of their feet and His promise that he'd meet someone who would buy shoes for the whole family. The story of God's care was more of a blessing than the shoes. It's a story that has become part of their testimony of God's love and faithfulness, a story they love to tell anyone who will listen, and a story of God's incredible grace to me.

ALL SHAPES AND SIZES

As we've said, generosity isn't limited to giving to the church. God has called us to be "lights in the world," which means people are looking to see who we are and how we care for others. Let me share three stories about desperately needed and creative giving.

First: In 1969, Hal Donaldson was twelve years old with three younger siblings. His Dad was a pastor, and one night, his parents were scheduled to attend a pastors' meeting. The babysitter was late. When she finally arrived, Hal's mom and Dad rushed out the door. On the way to the meeting, their car was hit head-on by a drunk driver. Hal's Dad died at the scene, and his mom was critically injured. The police found their home address and sent officers to inform and help the children. As the neighbors saw the squad cars arriving at the Donaldsons' home, they quickly gathered on their porch. A police officer explained the devastating news that the father had died in the crash and their mother was severely hurt. Then he asked, "Who will care for these four children?"

The officer waited, and they all waited. No one spoke for what seemed to Hal like an eternity, but finally, Bill and Louvada Davis spoke up: "We'll take them."[49] The Davises were a family of six living in a single-wide mobile home. Of the couples standing on the porch that night, they probably had the fewest resources, but they had the biggest hearts. For nearly a year while their mom was in the hospital and rehab, the Donaldson kids lived with the Davises. It was cramped, but it was a loving home. Mr. and Mrs. Davis put clothes on their backs, food in their stomachs, and hope in their hearts.

Years later, Hal was a journalist. He remembered that he had been cared for at a critical season of his life by people who weren't related, who had very little space and money, but who loved them when no one else volunteered. God began to stir Hal's heart when he saw a migrant camp off I-5 in Northern California. He filled the back of a pickup and handed groceries to workers harvesting nearby crops. This simple seed of kindness and compassion has grown into Convoy of Hope, one of the tremendous humanitarian organizations in the world today. Convoy partners with businesses and local churches to provide aid in all types of natural disasters and crises. Wherever a calamity strikes, Convoy of Hope is among the first relief organizations to arrive and one of the last to leave.

The Davises were simply living with a heart to help their neighbors in a time of need. They never knew their act of kindness would result in more than 200 million people being served through the outreaches of Convoy of Hope. By sowing a sacrificial seed of love and compassion for the Donaldson family, God

---

49 Hal Donaldson and Kirk Noonan, *Your Next 24 Hours: One Day of Kindness Can Change Everything* (United States: Baker Publishing Group, 2017), 13.

brought a harvest of blessings into more lives than any one family could ever reach.

And the second story: Our nation's capital has two major newspapers. As we planned to have a Jammin' event there, a local leader offered to call and set up an appointment for me with the business director of one of the papers.

A day later, I had the meeting. When I walked into the offices, I was escorted to a conference room. A few minutes later, the business director walked in and introduced himself. Getting right to business, he asked about what we were doing and how he could help?

I explained the purpose of Jammin', that we were a Christian outreach to youth and families. We were working on a basketball tournament on Pennsylvania Avenue and our main event in the Wizard's arena. "We want to reach kids and their families to bring them hope."

I had no idea how he'd respond, and I was surprised when he smiled and told me, "Steve, I want you to know that I'm a Joseph for you." He let that sink in for a few seconds, and then he asked, "Do you know what that means?"

I answered, "I know what it means to me, but I'm not sure what it means to you."

He took a deep breath and explained, "I'm a person who has paid a high price for my faith. I've been rejected by my family, but like Joseph in Genesis, God has put me in the right place at the right time to make a difference. I'm here to help you. What do you need from me?"

I told him we have several levels of sponsorship, and I asked him to consider the "gold level." It only took seconds for him to reply, "That's seven full-page ads."

"Let me rephrase that," I explained. "We have a sponsorship for seven full-page newspaper ads."

He nodded, "You've got it."

My meeting with the business director included one of the most profound statements I've ever heard. Obviously, this man had wrestled with the meaning of his pain and rejection, and he had found that God was using even his heartaches to put him in a position to do good for the kingdom . . . just like Joseph, who had been betrayed by his brothers, falsely accused by Potiphar's wife, and forgotten in prison for many years. Yet God hadn't forgotten him. When the time was right, and when the situation required a special person, God used him to rescue two nations from starvation, the Egyptians and his own family.

And the third: A dear couple has been part of our church through thick and thin. When we were about to open our new building a few years ago, we couldn't afford a lot of the furnishings. We'd constructed the framework for a very nice kitchen, but there was no money for the appliances and other equipment. One day during this trying time, I saw a note had been slipped under my door. This couple included a check and explained, "We saved this money to remodel our kitchen, but God told us to take care of His house before we take care of ours. He wants us to put Him first. This is everything we've saved to fix up our kitchen. We hope this helps in the church's kitchen. We're giving this from our hearts."

OPEN HANDS, OPEN HEARTS

A generous heart doesn't depend on temperament, age, financial status, or any other external metric. It's all about responding to God's gracious gifts to us. Let me offer a few ideas and suggestions:

There's no harvest without sowing. I've talked to many people who are mildly to very upset with God because He seems to be too stingy with them. When I ask about their pattern of giving, they quickly insist they've given enough. That could be true. God isn't a vending machine who is obligated to pop out blessings when and how we want them. But quite often, people find all kinds of excuses to keep their money and hoard their time. I tell them, "Give God a shot. He asks us to test Him to see if He'll bless when we give. The ball is in your court. Test Him and see what happens."

Evaluate your risk tolerance. This concept is very familiar to investors and people in financial management, and it applies to all of us. Our willingness to give generously and even sacrificially is based on our trust in God's character. I believe God delights in surprising us with blessings when we take another step of faith.

A generous heart doesn't depend on temperament, age, financial status, or any other external metric. It's all about responding to God's gracious gifts to us.

Look for stepping stones of blessing. One leads to another. When you and I give, we set in motion a domino effect, a cascade of blessing, of God's intimate involvement in meeting the needs of others, expanding our impact, and bringing deep satisfaction and joy to us.

If I hadn't invested my time and a little money to buy the Cuban pastor shoes for him and his family, I wouldn't have been open to God's promise to do the same thing for me.

Craft your testimony. Your story of God's work in and through you is just as valuable as your other resources. Take time to outline what God did to draw you to himself, what happened at the point of salvation, and how He has changed your life since then. Your story doesn't have to compete with anyone else. Just tell it, tell it often, and tell it well.

Listen and respond. That's been the recurring message of this book, hasn't it? God loves us and wants to communicate His heart to us. When we follow His example of generosity, He delights in leading us again and again to move into the lives of people who desperately need His love, provisions, and power. Listen carefully to the whispers, let His Word guide you, and follow His leading.

A lot of people have it backwards: they think God demands that they give, and they feel resistant to give in to these demands. It's just the opposite: God has already poured out His heart, His love and forgiveness, and His blessings to us. The more we're amazed at His generosity, the more we'll see that partnering with Him through our giving is one of the greatest privileges of our lives.

> *"But whatever you do, find the God-centered, Christ-exalting, Bible-saturated passion of your life, and find your way to say it and live for it and die for it. And you will make a difference that lasts. You will not waste your life"*[50].
> —John Piper

---

50 John Piper, *Don't Waste Your Life* (Wheaton: Crossway, 2003), 47.

CHAPTER 9
LEGACY: PRESERV-ING THE CATCH

"God's real desire, in addition to displaying His glory, is to claim your heart and the hearts of those you love."[51]
—PRISCILLA SHIRER

Before every trip, Dad did two things to help me understand his perspective. He called me over and unrolled a chart. He pointed to the spot where we were going to fish so I'd appreciate how long it would take to get there. And then he said, "Steve, this is how God provides for our family. Let's put our hands on this chart and ask God to bless our trip and bring us home safe." Dad led me through this spiritual affirmation before every trip.

Dad treated me with respect, and sometimes more respect than I wanted. Shortly after he taught me the lesson about tithing God's crew share, he announced one day, "Steve, you're a working man now, and men who have jobs take on more responsibility. Your mother and I will provide a roof over your head and food at

51 Priscilla Shirer, *Fervent: A Woman's Battle Plan to Serious, Specific and Strategic Prayer* (United States: B&H Publishing Group, 2015) , 22.

our table, but from this day on, you need to buy your clothes and pay for your entertainment. You'll pay for fun times with your friends. In all of this, you'll learn to make good decisions about money. I have confidence in you."

I became convinced Dad was serious about my new level of responsibility as we finished a tuna trip and docked in Astoria, Oregon, to sell our fish. He called my mom to let her know we'd be there for a few days to sell the fish, and she brought my two sisters along so the family could spend some time together before Dad and I went out again. When my mom and sisters arrived, we all went out to dinner together. When we were finished with our meal, Dad told the waiter, "Two checks, please." He nodded toward me and said, "My son will pay for his meal."

I wanted to say, "Really? You're not going to pay for my dinner? My sisters have been having fun with their friends while I've been working, but you're going to pay for their meal and not mine?" It hurt my feelings … but not as much as it hurt my mom's. It took a while, but I finally realized that my father was teaching me one of the most valuable lessons: to stand on my own two feet, trust God to provide, and use what He gave me wisely. (My mom got over it, too.)

With insights that apply to every sphere of life, Patrick Lencioni comments, "If everything is important, then nothing is."[52] Something has to be most important.

That's true, isn't it? It certainly is true for anyone who yearns to live a life of purpose and meaning. My parents placed that priority of modeling a life of faith and love.

---

52 Patrick Lencioni, *Silos, Politics, and Turf Wars* (San Francisco: Jossey-Bass, 2006), p. 17.

Dad seldom if ever taught me lessons like a professor teaching students, but he taught me plenty as I worked with him and watched him in every conceivable situation. He exemplified the instructions given to the people of Israel by Moses when he led them out of Egypt:

*Hear, O Israel: The L*ORD *our God, the L*ORD *is one. Love the* L*ORD *your God with all your heart and with all your soul and with all your strength. These commandments that I give you today are to be on your hearts. Impress them on your children. Talk about them when you sit at home and when you walk along the road, when you lie down and when you get up. Tie them as symbols on your hands and bind them on your foreheads. Write them on the doorframes of your houses and on your gates.*
—Deuteronomy 6:4–9

In every way and every day, Dad impressed biblical principles on me.

Dad imparted the concept of stewardship onto me. He explained, "As a fisherman, I never know what the next season will bring. It could be fantastic or we might come back with fewer fish than we had hoped. Either way, I'm responsible to take care of our family. After a good season, I need to save some money in case the next year isn't as productive. I can't spend it all and just hope things will work out." But Dad didn't stop there. He had a lesson for me. He said, "Steve, you need to be a good steward of what God entrusts to you. When we come back from a trip, if I see you throwing money away on things that don't matter, the amount of money you made on that trip will be the cap of what you'll make the next trip. When you prove that you're a good steward of your income, taking care of your money and honoring God with your giving, there will be no limit on what you can earn." That's the reason I invested in a new duplex instead of buying a Porsche Carrera.

YOUR PRIORITY: LEAVING A LEGACY

Legacy doesn't just happen—you have to want it, envision it, speak spiritual truth into the lives of those you love, and model what you're talking about. Most of you won't have the opportunity to spend forty days at sea with just your dad or your family, but you can plant a legacy right where you are. If you have children, you know what your legacy will be. If you don't have children, ask God to put some people on your heart so you can pour into their lives. No matter who you invest in, the goal is the same: to provide an environment and encouragement for them to experience the wonder of God's grace and greatness, so they'll make Him their highest priority.

I've lived with a sense of gratitude for how I was raised, and I've looked for ways to give my family the best opportunities to experience God's presence and to have shared markers in our lives. In the years that I traveled as an evangelist, I would often take one of our kids with me alone on a trip. They have crazy stories to tell of Dad juggling responsibilities, but our time together was unforgettable. Janelle will always remember me trying to fix her hair as a little girl and getting the right shoes on. For Jordan, it's the trip we shared traveling together to Indonesia. I loved seeing his heart of compassion as we spent time with kids living in a garbage dump in Jakarta. As I've mentioned, our older son Josh and his wife serve on our pastoral team at Eastridge. Many times, when Josh was just a boy, he would volunteer to take a day trip with me when I preached in a nearby church. What could have been lost moments became foundational—for them and for me. Today, it's a true gift to see Josh and Carrie leading their family and serving as key leaders in our church.

> The moments when you speak words that bring hope and encouragement to a hurting person are the acts that will endear you to people and lead them to consider the Jesus you serve.

God will show you ways that you can invest yourself into the lives of your kids. It begins by modeling a legacy of love. One scripture that you can glean so much from is Ephesians 5:33 "Each one of you also must love his wife as he loves himself, and the wife must respect her husband." Take to heart the lifelong imprint of loving your spouse in front of your kids, and ask the Holy Spirit to lead and empower you to impart grace, forgiveness, love, and respect to each other.

Legacy isn't about accumulating stuff; it's about investing in others. The seeds of love, compassion, and generosity will grow to bless and change the people God has placed in your life.

Legacy is about giving and sharing your life and your blessings with others. The moments when you speak words that bring hope and encouragement to a hurting person are the acts that will endear you to people and lead them to consider the Jesus you serve.

Just as worship that costs you nothing really isn't worship, legacy that costs you nothing really isn't legacy. Legacy only comes to life when you're willing to sacrifice for someone else's success. Mark Batterson put it this way, "Legacy isn't measured by what we accomplish in our lifetimes. It's measured by our coaching tree, our mentoring chain. It's measured by the fruit we grow on other people's trees. It's measured by the investments we make in others that are still earning compound interest twenty years later. It's measured by every blessing we bestow."[53]

PRESERVING THE CATCH

In these pages, I've described the importance of a great crew and investing in the best bait and gear, but one of the most important aspects of fishing is preserving the catch. Halibut are sold as a fresh fish, so they have to be kept on ice. As a fisherman, you can make a lot more money by delivering your fish to market in Seattle rather than Alaska, but making this long run means guaranteeing the fish are in excellent condition and that the fish hold has enough ice to make it to the warmer waters on the trip south.

On one trip, we came into port in Alaska with our boat completely loaded with fish. The weather was good, and the conditions were right to make the run to Seattle and capitalize on the higher price, but it meant we had to go the extra mile to preserve the fish. We opened the main hatch and pulled out a few thousand pounds of fish that we sold in the Alaskan port. We needed to

---

53 Mark Batterson, *Double Blessing: Don't Settle for Less Than You're Called to Bless* (United States: Multnomah, 2019), 13.

create enough space so we could lay ice between the top of the fish and the roof of the fish hold. Then we had the dock crew shoot a ton of fresh ice onto our deck.

Chris and I had on our full rain gear and special pullover wrist protection to keep the slime from going up our sleeves. Slime is actually a very important natural preservative for the fish, but it's not so great for us. I was ready for one of the dirtiest jobs you can imagine: I lay flat on the top layer of fish, and Chris pushed me by my boots deeper into the hold so I could throw fresh ice to the furthest edges. In just a few feet, I hit the first pocket of chilled ice water and slime—it went all over my face and beard, then slid down the inside of my raingear. When I finished a section, Chris pulled me back out by my boots and helped me ice another area. Each time was the same slimy mess. Though the hold was refrigerated, it had to be a temperature where the fish wouldn't freeze, so as the fish moved around with the rolling of the sea, a little water and slime created pockets. Finally, we were done. We had spread ice to all the corners and all edges. We then laid a cover of ice across the top, and the crew helped us put the main hatch back on.

Chris and I were the only crew members who went into the hold, and we were covered in slime inside and outside of our rain gear. We just wanted it off! We were already headed to Seattle at full speed, so we asked my Dad to slow down the boat. He wasn't too happy about it because we were passing outside Glacier Bay and traveling in the gray glacier water of Icy Strait. He finally gave in for what he knew would be a quick stop. The boat slowed down, and Chris jumped in just ahead of me. I saw his face come bursting to the surface—he was gasping for air in the frigid water. I jumped in before I changed my mind. It was a jolt to hit the water, and soon I was racing to catch my breath and scramble back to the boat. The cook handed us some warm, fresh water to rinse off the salt water and a couple of towels. A few minutes later, we were on deck, ready for a hot drink and wheel watch as we cruised south.

> Don't give up on a son or daughter who is far from God. The most valuable catch is seeing salvation in the lives of the people God places in your life.

It was messy and miserable in the moment and took a lot of effort and special care, but if we hadn't preserved the catch, all that we had worked for would have been lost. Never give up on a person because it is messy or painful. Don't give up on a son or daughter who is far from God. The most valuable catch is seeing salvation in the lives of the people God places in your life. Legacy presses through the pain and mess to risk for what matters the most.

FULL CIRCLE

When Paul and Barnabas split, the sad irony is that Paul didn't treat John Mark with the same generous spirit that Barnabas had shown toward Paul when the apostles doubted his new faith in Christ. At considerable risk to his own reputation, Barnabas gave Paul a chance to prove himself. Paul wasn't as gracious with John Mark . . . at least, not at that moment. I believe Paul thought about that bitter split for years, and later, he made up for his rash decision by welcoming John Mark back into the fold. At the very end of his action-packed life, Paul wrote his protégé, Timothy, "Get Mark and bring him with you, because he is helpful to me in my ministry" (2 Timothy 4:11).

We don't know if Barnabas learned of Paul's change of heart, but if he didn't then, he knows it now. Paul's legacy included deep, trusting relationships with elders and other believers wherever he went, and he had the courage to change his mind about a young man who had disappointed him years before.

But the New Testament clearly shows that Paul learned his lesson. Luke's account and Paul's letters show that Paul learned to be a mentor as well as a trailblazer. He had a profound impact on two men—Philemon the slave owner and Onesimus the runaway—and navigated reconciliation with consummate skill. He cared deeply for young pastors Timothy and Titus, and his heart broke when a trusted companion, Epaphroditus, was so sick Paul thought he might die. Perhaps the scene that illustrates Paul's shepherd's heart occurred when he traveled back to Jerusalem for the last time. He was in a hurry and didn't have time to stop at Ephesus, where he had spent three years teaching the Scriptures and sharing the gospel in that important port city. He asked the elders of the church to meet him at Miletus. His sense of purpose was as clear and fierce as ever. He told them, "I only know that in every city the Holy Spirit warns me that prison and hardships are facing me. However, I consider my life worth nothing to me; my only aim is to finish the race and complete the task the Lord Jesus has given me—the task of testifying to the good news of God's grace" (Acts 20:23-24). He encouraged them, warned them, and reminded them of their calling. "When Paul had finished speaking, he knelt down with all of them and prayed. They all wept as they embraced him and kissed him. What grieved them most was his statement that they would never see his face again. Then they accompanied him to the ship" (vv. 36-37). People don't weep and embrace someone who is harsh and uncaring. They only respond that way when they're deeply convinced of the person's affection. Paul's tenacity never wavered but became tempered with kindness, compassion, and genuine love.

If Paul's story had ended when he kicked Barnabas and John Mark off the team, we'd have a very different picture of the man and his impact. But it didn't end there. God softened Paul's heart, gave him patience with young leaders, and used him to equip them to carry the torch after he was executed in Rome.

Paul's legacy isn't that he traveled around to different cities, preached, and left. Everywhere he went, he appointed leaders so the impact would continue, deepen, and spread. In fact, if we look at only three people he mentored, we see the multiplied impact of his life—an impact that continues today. When Phoebe carried Paul's letter to the believers in Rome, they undoubtedly asked her to explain the concepts in the letter. In the most powerful city on earth, Phoebe left a legacy of truth explained. We get a clearer picture of Paul's impact on young leaders in his relationships with Timothy and Titus. As you might recall, Paul's experience in Lystra was perhaps the most checkered in his career. The people assumed he was a god because God used him to heal a crippled man, but not long after that, they tried to stone him to death. When Paul and Silas returned there to encourage the believers (a great act of faith if there ever was one!), Paul met Timothy. The Christians in the city were impressed with the young man's faith and faithfulness, and Paul asked Timothy to join his team. We have glimpses of Timothy's involvement in Paul's letters. In fact, Paul lists his protégé as a co-author in six of them. Paul poured his heart, his soul, and his strategic thinking into Timothy. When Timothy became the pastor of the church in Ephesus, Paul wrote two letters to him— letters which pastors have used as encouragement and guidance throughout the history of the church. Similarly, the letter to Titus also contains advice and instructions about leading a church, and it includes two of the most powerful and beautiful depictions of grace found in the Scriptures (Titus 2:11–14 and 3:3–8).

Paul may not have trusted John Mark enough to take him on the second trip to visit the churches, but he trusted Phoebe, Timothy, and Titus—mentoring them with grace, clarity, and power so they could follow his example. They had a front row seat to learn from the second greatest teacher in history!

THE LOOMING LEADERSHIP CHALLENGE

Paul and Barnabas's example of raising up the next generation of leaders is one we need today. Church leaders are warning of a leadership crisis on the horizon. Building a great church takes time, and the vast majority of our largest churches have been pastored by the same leader for over twenty years. It takes this time to build sacred trust, establish vision, and lead people to operate with high levels of faith.

However, as older leaders near the last years of their ministries, most of our churches aren't raising up the trained and anointed leaders to carry the baton forward. The success rate of handing off leadership is extremely disappointing and detrimental to the health of the church. I encourage you and your church leadership to develop plans that honor the leaders who have planted a seed of legacy into the body. At the same time, invest in healthy pathways that open doors for mentorship and development leadership from within your church. We desperately need next-generation leaders who share the DNA of the church, who have a fresh vision, and will lead the church to present Christ to a lost and dying world.

"What you do is your history. What you set in motion is your legacy."[54]
—Leonard Sweet

COMPARE AND CONTRAST

Allan Houston knows something about appreciating his father's legacy. Allan's Dad, Wade, grew up in Tennessee during severe racial discrimination. When Wade was ten years old, he and his father weren't allowed to attend any of the basketball games at the University of Tennessee because they were Black. Wade's legacy is one of faith in Christ. He answered God's call to move beyond the pain of man's failure to love. He dedicated himself to honor God and led his family with character and dignity. This commitment flowed into his love of basketball and empowered him through all the racial roadblocks he faced in coaching. His faith and grit were honored when he was selected as the first Black head coach

---

54 Leonard Sweet, *Soulsalsa: 17 Surprising Steps for Godly Living in the 21st* Century (United States: Zondervan, 2002)

of the University of Tennessee basketball team and the first Black head coach in the Southeastern Conference.

But the story gets even better. Allan had the great honor of playing for his Dad at UT. This gave him the unique opportunity to witness his Dad in pressure situations and see his character and his faithfulness to God. Allan and I have talked about the blessing of having loving Dads who saw us as their legacy, and we've talked about the responsibility to give our children the same incredibly powerful gift.

Allan went on from Tennessee to star in the NBA, becoming a two-time All-Star with the New York Knicks. He also won a gold medal with the USA Olympic basketball team.

Through all of his success, Allan concluded that one thing is most important: following God and leaving a legacy, first to his family and then to a broader circle. Allan has seven children and he's doing for them what his father did for him. Allan leads a ministry with the acronym FISLL as the title. The letters represent Faith, Integrity, Service, Leadership, and Legacy. Allan's message is, "Don't wait. Live your legacy right now." As parents, we can easily be preoccupied with conflict at home over money, control, and in-laws, and our minds can be inundated with hopes and fears about our careers. We can think, My kids are fine. I'll give them more attention later. Allan says, "Later is now! You're crafting your lifelong impact today. Don't miss it!"

Learn more about Allan Houston and FISLL.

The Most Valuable Catch

Some of us, like Allan and me, can easily see the positive impact our parents, especially our fathers, have had on us. When we think of God, we connect the dots between the love, direction, and protection we experienced in our earthly relationships with our Heavenly Father. Of course, God is infinitely more loving, wise, and powerful than any human being, but a strong relationship with our parents gives us a leg up on our concept of God. We can compare God with our dads, but many others can't make that comparison. Some of the NBA players who spoke at our Jammin' events told audiences about tough experiences growing up, including being abused or abandoned . . . and sometimes both. As they opened up and shared their journey of struggling for hope and wholeness, the arenas were frozen in silence as the moment shifted from a star player in front of his fans, to one human being sharing with another how they found what really matters the most. Their honesty and transparency broke down barriers and won the hearts of those listening.

These moments changed both the players and the fans. The players were changed by seeing God use them to help adults and kids reach for the grace and love of God that can heal and lift any heart. It was powerful to watch as players traveled to different cities, gave up other opportunities and never asked to be paid. They wanted this experience to be true worship back to God because of the profound work of grace He had performed in their hearts. Some would ask, are hurting people stuck in a hopeless cycle of pain, with the only option of leaving a destructive legacy to their kids? Not at all. They have to work harder to see the contrast between their parents and God.

People long for authenticity. These basketball players told personal stories of family disruption, alcoholism and addiction, financial hardships, a parent leaving, and never being seen again. But they also poured out their hearts, speaking of how people shared hope with them and modeled the love of God that transformed their lives. They spoke passionately about what Christ had done in their lives and challenged young people to believe the same for theirs. I'm convinced that their honesty was perhaps the most important reason God used Jammin' in such powerful ways.

We were more lost than we could ever imagine, but in Christ, we're loved more deeply than we could possibly hope.

King David was one of the most remarkable leaders in history, but his story starts in a deep, dark hole. When the prophet Samuel came to his house to anoint the new king of Israel, David's Dad lined up all of his sons . . . all except David. His father didn't consider him important enough to be included! And when David was sent to King Saul's camp to take food for his brothers who were in the army, his brothers mocked him as worthless. They must have been shocked when he walked out to the plain to kill the giant Goliath! In one of his psalms, David reflected on the contrast between his parents and God. He reminded himself that God is trustworthy, strong, and loving, and he saw God as beautiful. But the wounds of the past were still with him. He pleaded with God:

> *Hear my voice when I call, LORD; be merciful to me and answer me. My heart says of you, "Seek his face!" Your face, LORD, I will seek. Do not hide your face from me, do not turn your servant away in anger; you have been my helper. Do not reject me or forsake me, God my Savior. Though my father and mother forsake me, the LORD will receive me. Teach me your way, LORD; lead me in a straight path because of my oppressors.*—Psalm 27:7–11

The struggle for David and many others among us was to believe God is very much unlike his parents, but he was convinced that even though his parents had forsaken him, the Lord would embrace him.

Whether we compare our parents with God or contrast them, the Spirit of God longs to transform us from the inside out, reminding us that the Father loves us so much that He sent Jesus to do what we couldn't do for ourselves. We were more lost than we could ever imagine, but in Christ, we're loved more deeply than we could possibly hope.

BEHIND THE SCENES

Luke doesn't tell us what happened with Barnabas after he and John Mark parted from Paul, but it doesn't take much to imagine the story. Barnabas stepped into people's lives when they were on the outside looking in, when other people doubted them, and when their stories could have faded into oblivion. After the painful split with Paul, I can imagine Barnabas pouring his life into John Mark, helping heal the wounds of failure and rejection, and instilling a new sense of purpose and calling in the young man. At some point, Peter comes back into the picture, and he became John Mark's friend and mentor. The Gospel of Mark is basically a compilation of Peter's stories and sermons about his time with Jesus. It may have been the first Gospel account written, and Matthew and Luke may have used it as the basis for their Gospels. John Mark's contribution to the early church, then, was enormous. (Not bad for a guy who had been a castoff.)

John Mark could have dropped entirely from the scene, but Barnabas's love, encouragement, and faith in the young man gave him a new future. What was Barnabas's impact for Christ? His legacy includes two men of very different temperaments—Paul and John Mark—who desperately needed someone to believe in them at critical moments in their lives. He didn't jockey for power and position in the early church, and he didn't demand to call the shots because he had given so generously to the cause. He just loved people, especially hurting people, and he made a profound difference in the trajectory of God's people.

In a picture of glorious redemption, God restored Paul's relationship with John Mark. Luke doesn't give us any information about it, but as we've seen, Paul does. As he penned his last words, anticipating death, Paul asked Timothy to bring John Mark to him. What prompted the change of heart? I can only imagine that Barnabas's tenacious love and encouragement picked John Mark off the ground when Paul discarded him, and he provided enough support and instruction so that John Mark finally proved himself . . . even to Paul.

Few of us can be a Paul, but all of us can be a Barnabas. My father poured himself into me as Barnabas did for John

Mark. God has called, energized, and challenged me to live like Barnabas. To the best of my ability, I want to pour myself out for my family, my friends, our board, the people of our church, and those in my community. Will you take this challenge in your life?

LEGACY BEGINS HERE

Fishing with my father gave me some of the most beautiful and exciting moments I could have imagined. In the earliest light of dawn, we watched a pod of humpback whales breaching one after the other off the coast of Alaska. On a trip fishing for tuna in much warmer waters, I swam with a massive school of porpoises, many of them coming in for a close look at the strange creature that was swimming so slowly. I vividly remember hauling in huge halibut and needing help to wrestle them onto the hatch. I have rich memories of standing on the deck with my Dad in storms that would make anyone quake in their rain gear. Those desperate and daring moments, too, are part of my Dad's legacy in my life.

Of all the wonderful times fishing with Dad, one of my favorites is a time when we were headed home to surprise the family with one of the biggest loads of fish we'd ever caught. We entered the Strait of Juan de Fuca just as the sunset was painted in glowing yellows, oranges, and reds. The skies were clear, and the water was calm. The boat was so full that the deck was barely above the waterline. As we entered the Strait, the captains of smaller, gill-net boats saw us pass by. Many of them knew my Dad because he had fished gill nets earlier in his career. In that beautiful moment, Dad received a hero's welcome as all the boats honked their horns, and fishermen waved and gave him a thumb's up. The radio on board lit up as one friend after another called to congratulate Dad on his success. He had stepped up to the next level of fishing—with the increased risks and the promise of greater rewards—and had made it.

That evening, I don't think any son could have been more proud of his father. His life inspired all those fishermen who celebrated his success, but most of all, he inspired me.

My father's methods may have been somewhat different from how most Dads treat their sons, but as I look back, I wouldn't change a thing. He imparted the most valuable lessons a young man could ever learn. The curriculum was sometimes hard, but I never doubted that he was a loving, kind, and wise teacher. I am who I am today because of my father's influence.

LEGACY BEGINS WITH YOU

In these chapters, I've described the impact of my Dad on my life, but you need to know more about the backstory. When my mom was growing up, she endured tremendous pain in a home with an alcoholic father. Sometimes, when her father came home drunk and didn't find the family there, he flew into a rage. He yanked out dresser drawers and poured the kids' clothes out on the lawn in front of the neighbors. At other times when he came home, and the food on the table wasn't what he wanted, he turned the table over and dumped the food on the floor. While her mom tried to salvage the food, he drove to his favorite bar and ate what he wanted. The rest of the family endured plenty of days of fear and uncertainty.

One day my mom's friend invited her to a church service. It seemed crazy, but she went. There she heard the message of Jesus and His love for her. The message seemed too good to be true, but she walked forward for prayer and decided to accept Christ. She later met a young soldier just getting out of the military. She shared her faith, and he, too, came to know the Lord. Not long after that, they were married, and as a newlywed couple chose to make Christ the center of their lives and marriage. Neither of them had a family that knew the Lord or demonstrated how to honor him, but together they were determined to start a legacy of faith in their life together.

Because my mom felt the prompting of the Lord and took the step of faith to accept Christ, it not only changed her, but it changed my father. When I came along, she planted the seeds of love and compassion in me for hurting people. She taught me to pray in the moment and listen to the prompts of the Holy Spirit.

> # Grace is greater than any broken place, and a new legacy of faith can start with you!

The greatest blessing in my life is that God has given our family a legacy of faith and grace. It's a legacy I want to build upon every day.

You may be hurting and believing you're beyond God's forgiveness and grace. You may feel that you've made so many mistakes that your opportunities are gone. I want to speak life into your heart and hope for your soul. God has you reading this book, so you can know His love for you is greater than any sin or mistake. Grace is greater than any broken place, and a new legacy of faith can start with you!

BEGIN AGAIN TODAY

I'm convinced that God wants to do something magnificent in each of our lives. Isaiah described the calamity of God's people being conquered by foreigners, but he told them that they should trust Him ...

... till the Spirit is poured on us from on high, and the desert becomes a fertile field, and the fertile field seems like a forest. The LORD's justice will dwell in the desert, his righteousness live in the fertile field. The fruit of that righteousness will be peace; its effect will be quietness and confidence forever. My people will live in peaceful dwelling places, in secure homes, in undisturbed places of rest. —Isaiah 32:15-18

Let me offer a few suggestions about trusting God to give us a powerful and positive legacy:

STUDY THE COMPARISON OR CONTRAST

Children instinctively make the connection between the most powerful and present people in their lives, their parents, and God ... for good or ill. Even as adults, those ideas are still "imprinted" on our hearts. It's wise to take stock of where our concepts of God originated. We may find that our faith is a direct result of our parents' love and support, but many of us have a very different story. It's time to ask God for wisdom and move into a process of forgiving and healing.

KEEP LEARNING

No matter how wonderful our parents may have been (and may still be), they will always be a faint image of the wonder of God's greatness and grace. We can spend the rest of our lives plumbing the depths of His character and His good intentions toward us.

IT'S NEVER TOO LATE

I've talked to men and women who have lived with deep wounds and regrets for decades. Many of them have given up on changing the course of their most important relationships, but I encourage them that it's never too late. Talk to a pastor, counselor, or wise friend, and trust the Spirit of God to do a deep work in you . . . and in the hearts of the people who need just as much grace and restoration.

Sharing time with my father was worth far more than my crew share. It was a treasure more valuable than gold. I recall an instance when we saw silhouettes of warships when we were a thousand miles off the coast of California. We were anxious because we weren't sure who they belonged to. Today, millions of young people are growing up without knowing who they belong to. They're desperate for love, for meaning, for connection. If we don't provide those essentials, they'll look somewhere else. It's our task and our calling as Christians to create an environment where everyone—those from solid backgrounds and those from shattered homes—can find their true identity as children of the King, deeply loved, completely forgiven, totally accepted, and called to a purpose far more significant than themselves.

We simply can't afford to mess that up. So listen for the Holy Spirit's prompts and reach for the most valuable catch.

"The greatest legacy one can pass on to one's children and grandchildren is not money or other material things accumulated in one's life, but rather a legacy of character and faith."[55]

—Billy Graham

55 *Focus on the Family*, Twitter Post, February 21, 2018, 6:59 AM.

Jammin' Against the Darkness

AVAIL +

AVAIL
PODCAST

THE AVAIL PODCAST

HOSTED BY VIRGIL SIERRA